FIVE FAIR RIVERS

Five Fair Rivers

Sailing the James, York, Rappahannock,
Potomac, and Patuxent

ROBERT DE GAST

THE JOHNS HOPKINS UNIVERSITY PRESS
BALTIMORE AND LONDON

FOR MY GRANDCHILDREN

Alden, Dyson, Karsyn, Kenneth, Kirstin, and Tyler, sailors all.

They'll inherit the boat. I hope they'll inherit the rivers.

© 1995 Robert de Gast
All rights reserved. Published 1995
Printed in the United States of America on acid-free paper
04 03 02 01 00 99 98 97 96 95   5 4 3 2 1

Maps prepared by Bill Nelson

The Johns Hopkins University Press
2715 North Charles Street
Baltimore, Maryland 21218-4319
The Johns Hopkins Press Ltd., London

ISBN 0-8018-5079-7

41330 ᴵₙᵍᵣₐₐ 1/96

Library of Congress Cataloging-in-Publication Data will be found at the end of this book.
A catalog record for this book is available from the British Library.

CONTENTS

FIVE FAIR RIVERS

On the west side of the Bay, wee said were 5. faire and delightfull navigable rivers, of which wee will nowe proceed to report.

—John Smith, *Description of Virginia,* 1612

The Plan

It is laughable, this business of moving around a small quarter of the world in one's own boat. It is maddeningly slow, frightening, strange, dull, uncomfortable, lovely, inconvenient, revelatory and undignified — all in the right proportions. It teaches you about a world you'd never guessed at when you were on land, and makes you obsessively alert to distinctions invisible to the people you've left behind there. It turns you into a creature of luck and weather. It shortens your horizon and makes you live by the minute and the hour. It grants you a floating detachment (sometimes serene and sometimes appalled) from the land on the beam. But it is the silliest possible way of getting to Brighton, if getting to Brighton was ever the point of the thing.

— Jonathan Raban, *Coasting,* 1987

The idea for a book on the rivers of the western shore of the Chesapeake came about, in a roundabout way, as a result of a solo circumnavigation I made years ago of the eastern shore of the bay, of which I wrote in *Western Wind, Eastern Shore.* A book review in *Cruising World* mentioned in passing that I had sold the little boat that I had sailed on that cruise and had acquired a thirty-five-foot ketch, "which undoubtedly draws more water." The reviewer continued, "Maybe he'll next celebrate the Western Shore, with its deeper rivers and higher land, which the Colonists long ago recognized as better cruising territory for that inevitable bigger boat." An idea was planted. And an apt quotation from Captain John Smith about the western shore's "5. faire and delightfull navigable rivers" provided the focus.

After that "inevitable bigger boat" that drew nearly six feet, there were a number of other vessels, before I finally settled, more than a decade later, on a Dovekie, with its four-inch draft, for the suggested project. It was true that the rivers on the other side of the bay were deeper than the creeks and marshes on the Eastern Shore, but I didn't need a deep-keel boat to explore them. It was much more interesting to sail in the shallows, close to shore, no matter how deep the middle.

I could not take the time to make a continuous voyage; I had to split the adventure into five separate cruises (*Fiddler*'s trailerability facilitated this approach) in five separate months. I would start in the spring, in April or May, with the James River, and make my last cruise, on the northernmost river, the Patuxent, in the fall—late September or early October. This plan would yield a variety of seasons and weather conditions.

I worried about the best approach. Should I go up the rivers? Down the rivers? Up one and down the next? Since all the rivers are tidal, there would be no advantage in sailing downriver: the current would reverse itself every six hours or so. In the end, I chose to go up the rivers. It seemed more natural, somehow, and in keeping with the notion of exploring. After all, the first reports of the rivers came from sailors who had journeyed up them looking for a passage to the Indies. Four hundred years later, I was merely following in their wake. But unlike them, I wanted to sail the rivers alone.

"A small yacht's cabin," Samuel Morison wrote, "is not only a home away from home and a floating camp; it is a little, closed-in world where you are free from all anxieties, problems and considerations except the primitive ones of keeping dry, warm and well fed. It is a little space walled off just for you . . . into which you retire after enjoying a day of the most divine form of movement ever invented by man."

A little, six-hundred-pound, double-ended sharpie would be my home for many weeks, and I had very limited space. I decided against taking an ice chest, both for reasons of space and because ice would be difficult to obtain on many parts of the rivers. Here's a list of everything I had with me on *Fiddler* during my cruises:

In the bow, I carried an eight-pound Bruce anchor, a few feet of chain, one hundred feet of anchor line, a small paddle, and two dock lines. In the starboard storage bin I carried a two-burner propane stove; two pots and a small skillet; enough groceries for a week; cooking implements, cutlery, and a couple of plates, mugs, and bowls; and a roll of paper towels. The port storage bin contained a sleeping bag; a few books; charts; a notebook; a small "point-and-shoot" camera; insect screens; a flashlight; two towels; and clothing.

Above the storage bins were stowed a self-inflating mattress and a pillow, two PVC pipes to support my "tent," and two ten-foot oars. Underneath the cockpit seat I stored a bucket, a lifejacket, the "back porch" cockpit tent, a swimming ladder, and a two-and-a-half-gallon water jug. In the lazaret I hid a small gas tank. A plastic solar shower bag was stowed on the stern under the tiller and would, on sunny days, deliver warm, and sometimes hot, water.

In other containers I kept a small weather radio receiver, tools, extra rope, cleaning materials, and toiletries. It was amazing how few supplies, and how little equipment, I needed to live, comfortably, for a week.

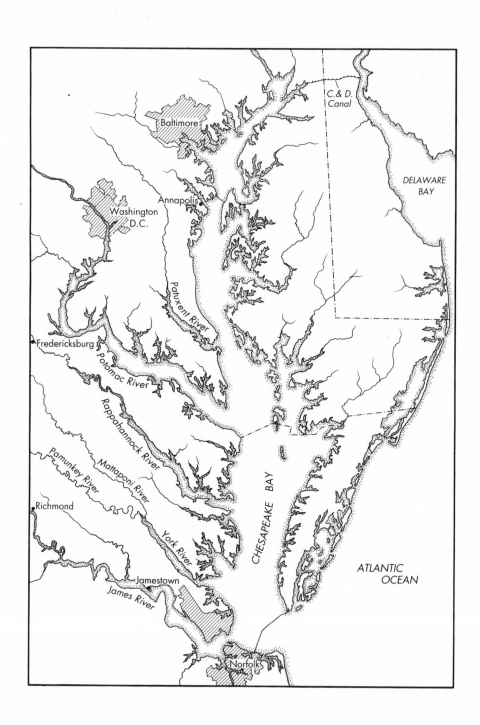

The Chesapeake Bay and Its Rivers

Within is a country that may have the prerogative over the most pleasant places of Europe, Asia, Africa, or America, for large and pleasant navigable rivers: heaven and earth never agreed better to frame a place for mans habitation.

—John Smith, *Description of Virginia*, 1612

The Chesapeake Bay never lacked for superlatives. Seldom has a region evoked such lyrical responses from its discoverers and settlers. "I was almost ravished at the first sight thereof," wrote George Percy, in the first communication from Virginia, in 1607. The letters and reports that were sent back to England were sometimes so exuberant that they provoked skepticism: they were thought to be the exaggerated ramblings of people who had never traveled anywhere, designed to increase confidence in the management of the Virginia Company and stimulate even greater investment. Life at Jamestown might be a "miserable distresse," but nobody complained about the Chesapeake. Wrote John Smith in a frequently quoted passage, "The mildnesse of the aire, the fertilitie of the soile, and the situation of the rivers are so propitious to the nature and use of man as no place is more convenient for pleasure, profit, and mans sustenance."

Although in the late fifteenth and early sixteenth centuries a number of explorers, among them Vespucci, Cabot, and Verrazano, likely sailed past the entrance to the Chesapeake Bay, none reported the bay's existence: perhaps it was night, perhaps there was fog, perhaps they were too far offshore.

In 1570, however, Spanish missionaries, members of the Society of Jesus, sailed from Santa Elena, in what is now South Carolina, and entered a bay they called Bahía de Madre de Dios. Juan de la Carrera was an eyewitness:

> Our Fathers and Brothers disembarked in a great and beautiful port, and men who have sailed a great deal and have seen it say it is the best and largest port in the world. So, if I remember rightly, the pilot remarked to me, It is called the Bay of the Mother of God, and in it there are many deep-water ports, each better than the next.

This was the first description of the Chesapeake, and the first reference to its rivers.

The rivers especially intrigued the early settlers. At first the rivers were seen as possible routes to the fabled Indies, the elusive Northwest Passage. In 1608 Captain John Smith, in two separate voyages, spent a considerable time sailing up many of the rivers, having earlier gone up the James, and having seen, while in captivity, the York and the Rappahannock. As the settlements around the Chesapeake grew, the rivers became important as watery highways, as fisheries, and sometimes as sewers.

Today the bay's dimensions remain roughly the same as they were ten thousand years ago, although its waters are shallower than they were before half the drainage basin was denuded of trees. The Chesapeake is still nearly two hundred miles long, and varies in width from three to thirty miles. Its watershed covers sixty-four thousand square miles, spread over six states and the District of Columbia. Almost 15 million people live in its drainage basin. Three of its rivers—the Susquehanna, the James, and the Potomac—are among the hundred largest in North America. The bay contains 18 trillion gallons of water, some of it fresh, some as salty as the ocean. The Chesapeake is an estuary, a place where salt and fresh water mix; it is the largest estuary in the United States, which boasts of 850.

The Chesapeake Bay is the drowned valley of the Susquehanna River. It is a young estuary, the product of dramatic climatic changes that began twenty thousand years ago, when most of eastern North America was covered by a huge glacier; and it settled into its present form roughly ten thousand years ago. As global warming increased, melting ice raised the water level in the oceans, and the inundation of the continental shelf began. During that eon the Atlantic coastline moved about seventy miles westward, to its present position. Sea level was more than three hundred feet lower than it is today.

The water level continues to rise, even today, perhaps an inch every one hundred years, owing in part to further melting of polar glaciers and in part to subsidence, the continual settling of the earth. The Chesapeake is not very deep: scientists have calculated its average depth at twenty-eight feet. There are, however, some very deep natural channels in the bay, and in several spots its depth exceeds one hundred feet.

Stone and Blanchard's *Cruising Guide to the Chesapeake* states categorically that "no cruising waters in the United States have more to offer the boatman than Chesapeake Bay." A great deal of the attraction of the bay lies in its rivers. Two of the earliest yachtsmen to explore the bay—George Barrie Jr. and his brother Robert—wrote, in a turn-of-the-century book called *Cruises Mainly in the Bay of the Chesapeake,* "The Bay would lose a large part of its fascination if there were no long rivers to explore." Perversely, although the Barrie brothers sailed the bay for many seasons as far south as Hampton Roads, they never explored any of the rivers beyond the anchorages at their mouths.

There are a lot of so-called rivers on the Chesapeake. If you count those actually named on the charts, there are precisely sixty-six. But most of those are really creeks, while others are more like sounds, or bays, and a few are more like ditches, guts, or sloughs.

The classic *Rivers of the Eastern Shore,* by Hulbert Footner, was subtitled *Seventeen Maryland Rivers,* and featured fine tales about the Pocomoke, the Choptank, the Wye, the Sassafras, the Chester, and a dozen others. "As rivers go," wrote Footner, "they are small affairs." Forty-six of the Chesapeake's named rivers are on the western shore, and six of them are no small affairs. Five of them, the James, the York, the Rappahannock, the Potomac, and the Patuxent, are navigable for very long distances. The sixth, the Susquehanna, although navigable for long stretches by the Indians in their canoes, could not be sailed by the deep-draft European ships and was therefore left off the list when Smith counted his "5. faire . . . rivers."

There are, of course, many other well-known rivers on the western shore: the Piankatank, South, West, and Severn Rivers, and the Magothy, the Bush, and the Gunpowder. But even the well-known, deep-dredged Patapsco, gateway to Baltimore harbor, is only eight miles long.

Ninety percent of the fresh water that daily flows into the bay comes from the James, the York, the Rappahannock, the Potomac, and the Susquehanna. The Patuxent supplies only a tiny portion of the bay's fresh water, and the relatively small volume of its water flow accounted for the early and drastic shoaling that occurred in its upper reaches within one hundred years of settlement. Even the broad Potomac saw dredging as early as 1800 between Georgetown and Alexandria.

The Chesapeake, "bless'd with many brave Rivers," was also cursed with them. The rivers became convenient sewers for the industries and settlements that were located on them, and most of the troubles of the bay can be traced directly to the rivers. Or rather, to the people that use them. From a few thousand natives, 105 people in Jamestown, and "neere 200. people" in Saint Marys City, the population along the shores of the bay and its rivers grew in 350 years to many millions. The Indians were not to share in that explosive growth: already in 1705 Robert Beverley could write, "The *Indians* of *Virginia* are almost wasted."

Land was thought to be "improved" if it was cleared and built upon. In fact, the land was only altered. The places along the rivers which are the most cherished are "unimproved": a narrow tree-lined stretch on the James, huge boulders along the Potomac, a marshy vista across the Patuxent, a sloping beach on the York, a towering cliff on the Rappahannock. "They're not making any more of it," developers say when praising the value of river frontage. If we could say, "They're not *taking* any more of it," we could still have some of the rivers' solitude and beauty to share with our grandchildren.

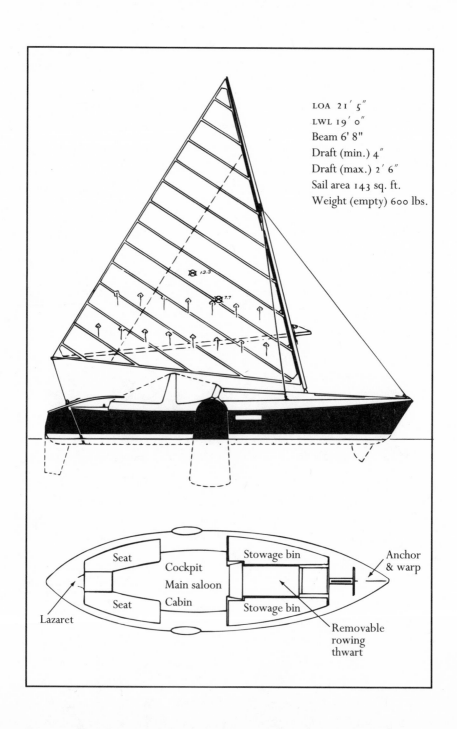

LOA 21' 5"
LWL 19' 0"
Beam 6' 8"
Draft (min.) 4"
Draft (max.) 2' 6"
Sail area 143 sq. ft.
Weight (empty) 600 lbs.

Seat

Cockpit
Main saloon
Cabin

Stowage bin

Stowage bin

Anchor & warp

Seat

Lazaret

Removable rowing thwart

The Boat

In essence the sharpie is a long skiff with sails. It is probably the most boat for the least expense, the easiest to build, and the most uncomplicated to rig and sail.

—Douglas Alvord, *On the Water,* 1988

Dovekie is the common name in North America for the little auk, a starling-sized member of the *Alcidae* family. Roger Tory Peterson described dovekies as "duck-like sea birds with stubby necks. They have a buzzy flight and a straddle-legged look when about to land." Elsewhere in his *Field Guide to the Birds,* Peterson called the dovekie "quite unlike anything else." The bird is found in prodigious numbers in the Arctic Circle and in North Atlantic waters.

Dovekie (rhymes with "love me") is also the name of a small boat that is "quite unlike anything else." At last count there were 152 Dovekies in the world, all but three in the United States. In the spring of 1987 I became the second owner of hull number 3, then already ten years old. Here's how it happened.

After twenty-five years of owning and sailing on dozens of boats in many parts of the world, I had come to the conclusion that I had invariably enjoyed myself most in small boats. Sure, it was thrilling to be able to sail, for a week, on America's largest sailboat, the Coast Guard's 295-foot bark *Eagle.* I had loved the year my wife and I spent aboard our thirty-five-foot cruising ketch *Qui Vive* in the Bahamas, and I had enjoyed spending time on a ninety-eight-foot schooner, making photographs for a story on what was then the most expensive charter boat in the Caribbean. But the most memorable sails had always been in small boats: a twenty-five-foot modified Soling on Finnish lakes; a twenty-two-foot

Sailmaster around the Delmarva Peninsula; a twenty-five-foot sharpie in Florida Bay. I started looking at small boats again.

In the mid-1980s I subscribed to *Small Boat Journal* and began following the unusual advertisements for an ultra-shoal-draft, lightweight, trailerable boat called the Dovekie, designed by Phil Bolger and built by a firm called Edey and Duff, in Mattapoisett, on Buzzards Bay, in Massachusetts. The ads, written by Peter Duff, were seductive and informative. At a time when most boatbuilders were selling space, speed, and status, Duff was rhapsodizing over a sort of seagoing tent with wings on the side, which had no bunks, no bilge, and—so far as I could see—no beauty. But he promised "absolutely trouble-free sailing and a cruising speed of 5½ miles per hour." I didn't run out and buy one, but I looked forward to Duff's advertising copy in each new issue of the magazine.

Bolger had referred to the hull shape of the Dovekie as being related to that of the sharpie. I had not known the term *sharpie* before, but discovered that the sharpie was *ur*-American in design, being a type of oyster dredger developed in the 1830s by the watermen around New Haven, Connecticut. Early sharpies had flat bottoms, a single, hard chine, and large, wooden centerboards. The dredge-boats were usually rigged with two freestanding masts; their sails were sprit-rigged. The maritime historian Howard Chapelle thought that the term *sharpie* came into use as early as 1857 "to distinguish between the sharp-bowed, flat-bottomed skiff and the scow; so 'sharpie' meant 'sharp-bowed.'" Flat-bottomed boats have served in fishing and transportation wherever practical considerations necessitated low-cost craft and shoal-water navigation.

In the summer of 1986, I found a book called *The Folding Schooner* aboard a thirty-five-foot sloop I was delivering from Annapolis to Martha's Vineyard. It was a collection of essays and boat plans by Philip Bolger, a brilliant, innovative naval architect. One of the chapters was devoted to the Dovekie, and during my off-watch hours I studied his drawings and read his comments.

Although all the design specifications for the other boats were listed in feet and inches, the Dovekie measured in at 6.52 meters by 1.82 meters. The Dovekie was designed in the metric system "at the request of the far-sighted Peter Duff, who wanted to break in himself and his crew to use it." The Dovekie, said Bolger, "is six-and-a-half meters long; never mind what it comes to in feet and inches." (It comes to a length of about twenty-one feet, five inches, and a width of five feet, eleven inches.) Having been brought up on the metric system, I was immediately intrigued by this aspect of the boat, although it clearly only had relevance to the boatbuilders.

The first Dovekie had been built in 1977 as a joint experiment by Bolger and the firm of Edey and Duff. This prototype was designed to be rowed by two or four people. The dead-flat bottom, Bolger wrote, was meant to give the boat maximal stability for her weight, and enough flat surface for four people to lie down. The resultant upright stance when aground, and the shallow, four-inch draft, were bonuses. By the time hull number 3 was built, the boat had gone through many changes, but Bolger's philosophy was intact:

> Dovekie is a strenuous attempt to produce a popular family recreational boat that will function without an engine. For this she plainly needed a high enough performance under sail, and tight enough control, to go under sail wherever there is wind and minimum space. Secondly, she must row well enough, in a calm, to make rowing her a mild satisfaction not leading quickly to frustration or exhaustion; this meant among other things that there could be no underwater surfaces or excrescences not absolutely necessary to float her, and that she must be as low to the water and streamlined as possible, certainly having no spars or wires sticking high in the air.

The production Dovekie hull, made of foam-cored fiberglass, weighs only about six hundred pounds, sails efficiently with two leeboards (a small centerboard in the bow was added in later models, and

I retrofitted my Dovekie with one), has a single, 143-square-foot sail that is sprit-rigged (carried on a mast that raises and lowers quickly and easily), and has a rowing port on each side.

In the fall of 1986, the *Small Boat Journal* carried three classified ads for used Dovekies. One was located in Texas, another in South Carolina. The third was closer to home:

> DOVEKIE, inboard jet engine, new reefing system, white hull, original owner, located on Long Island, $6,450.

I was mystified by the "jet engine" business, but I called the New York telephone number and spoke to the owner about his *Idler,* hull number 3. I voiced my interest, but other ventures and projects kept me from going to New York to look this Dovekie over.

Then, in February 1987, after having been out of the country for several months, I noticed that the same classified ad was still running in the magazine. I called again. The boat was still for sale. The owner complained that since he had begun running the ads, nobody had even looked at the vessel. It had been a rough, cold winter, and sailing, or buying an open boat, was far from everyone's mind.

Now, however, spring was only a few weeks off, and on the first weekend in March I drove from Virginia to Long Island. By the time I reached the Verrazano Bridge, at noon on Saturday, the temperature had reached seventy-two degrees—a record. It was clearly sailboat-buying weather.

After all the time I had spent looking at drawings and drooling over ad copy, I had not yet seen a Dovekie in the flesh, so to speak. But there she sat, on a trailer, in the backyard of her owner's country house, looking—well, *forlorn* is a kind word for how she looked. This was the weirdest-looking boat I'd ever seen. Her leeboards, of dark mahogany, were in grave contrast to her white, flush-deck hull. There was mildew inside the boat, and her spars needed varnishing, as did the oars and the leeboards. Time, and winter, had not been kind to the vessel. A tiny engine that was tucked away under a cockpit seat looked as though it had been built by Rube Goldberg. But the sail seemed in good shape, and the boat was so simple in rig and design that nothing much, aside from the cosmetic problems, could be wrong; in less than half an hour I had "surveyed" the little boat.

We negotiated, we argued, we cajoled, we bantered, we bartered, we agreed. Three hours after my arrival in Stony Brook I became the legal owner of a Dovekie called *Idler*. And the trailer. And the engine. Despite Bolger's "strenuous attempt to produce a . . . boat that will function without an engine," I had acquired a boat with an engine, an inboard engine.

Idler's owner, a New York investment banker, had used her on weekends, sailing the waters of eastern Long Island Sound. But his hectic schedule made depending on sail power or oar power undesirable, and, not wanting to disfigure the boat with the addition of an outboard engine, he decided to have a small inboard engine designed, built, and installed. Using the power-head of a 9.9-horsepower Johnson outboard, Wolfpak Marine in Seattle built a jet engine with an underwater intake flush with the hull. A water-jet exhaust, located near the stern, propelled the boat at five or six knots. With nothing protruding from the hull, and without a propeller, the boat could still move in five or six inches of water. The motor made an overwhelming noise and cost nearly as much as he had paid for the boat itself, but it let him get to Wall Street on Monday mornings.

The "infernal" combustion engine, roughly one cubic foot in size and weighing less than twenty pounds, sat discretely tucked away underneath the stern seat. It always started on the first pull of the cord, slurped about a gallon of gas per hour, and appeared to require no maintenance, but used the entire hull as a sound amplifier. When there was not enough wind to sail, rowing—or drifting—was infinitely preferable to using the motor, except under the most pressing circumstances.

Very late in the afternoon of that spring day, I trailered *Idler* back to the Chesapeake. I remember thinking, "If she sails as well as she trailers, this will indeed be 'an absolutely trouble-free boat.'" For the next three weeks, though, winter wouldn't relinquish its hold. But finally, in the first week of April, my wife, Evelyn, and I launched the boat at a ramp a mile from our house, and I rowed the Dovekie back to our pier. That afternoon, I brought the mast and sprit, newly varnished, aboard, and we went for a sail. The experience was sensational. The Dovekie went to windward well, tacked cleanly, was a hot performer on a reach, and was docile downwind. Her steering was uncannily precise. I was enthralled. Later that afternoon I started and ran the engine, and we measured her speed through the water. It was a noisy but exhilarating performance.

All of this echoed Bolger's contention:

> Everyone who has sailed her has been impressed. She is fast on all points, having for instance sailed thirteen nautical miles in two hours, nearly close-hauled, singlehanded, in choppy water. She's extraordinarily close-winded. . . . She's the most perfect boat to steer I've ever handled, razor-sharp and instant in response to every movement of the tiller, yet steady on course. . . . I wish I was sure how this thoroughbred behavior was produced, so I could count on delivering it on demand.

The leeboards, although somewhat awkward looking, turned out to be no problem at all. Leeboards were developed in the Netherlands in the early fourteenth century, and all the pictures in the history books when I was growing up in Holland showed boats with leeboards. Was there any other way to gain directional control? When the centerboard was invented, leeboards went out of fashion. But leeboards still had the advantage of being inexpensive to build and install and trouble-free to operate, and were really the only way in which a small boat could have an uninterrupted, flat bottom.

I had wanted to change *Idler*'s name from the moment I first saw the letters on the stern. There was precedent for *Idler:* the famous maritime historian Samuel Eliot Morison's thirty-foot yawl, designed by Sam Crocker and built in 1927, had been named *Idler*. Not bad, as company went, but the name did not feel right—for me. I wanted my new boat to seem a bit more energetic. But changing the name of a ship is universally acknowledged to bring bad luck. Jonathan Raban had tried to solve that problem in a very creative way. He had bought a ketch called *Gosfield Maid,* and as he related in *Coasting,* didn't like the name much: "It is famously unlucky to change a boat's name: you are pretty well guaranteed an early death by drowning. But it is permissible, as far as I know, to switch the letters about. Chuck GOSFIELD MAID into the air, let the pieces fall where they will, and they come out as DIE, DISMAL FOG."

He had decided against that alternative, but it gave me an idea. The possible permutations of the twenty-five conceivable combinations of the letters *i, d, l, e,* and *r,* at least in English, yielded only *Riled.* That also seemed inappropriate to my state of mind. I fooled around with the letters for some time, and then Evelyn suggested *Fiddler.* Perhaps adding only a few letters would bring only a little bad luck, she thought. So I decided to keep all the letters, and add two. The new name frequently reminded me how, in some circumstances, the Dovekie copied with perfection the sideways movement of the fiddler crab. And unlike aquatic crabs, fiddler crabs have both gills and primitive lungs, allowing them to survive in and out of water. Unlike many sailboats, *Fiddler* would be spending lots of time out of the water on her trailer.

It is common knowledge among sailors that the cost of boating only begins with the purchase of the vessel. One-fifth, and more, of the price of the boat is usually spent on accessories, gadgets, electronics, and safety gear. It was a revelation to me that I could own a perfectly seaworthy boat that didn't require a bosun's chair, an anchor winch, spare turnbuckles, or a depthfinder, and whose toolkit only contained two screwdrivers and three different wrenches—with which I could take everything on the boat, including the engine, completely apart.

The best boats, Bolger had once written, "are either big enough to live on, or small enough to take home." Someone else had written, "The best boat is the one that allows you to go sailing." *Fiddler* met both of those criteria.

In the next couple of years the Dovekie was trailered to destinations as far apart as Georgian Bay, in Ontario, and Cayo Costa, on Florida's west coast. We used her on weekends from early spring to late fall around the Chesapeake, or on hour-long sunset sails after work on weekdays. Getting the boat ready for a sail only took minutes and involved nothing more than packing a picnic cooler and a change of clothing. "The success of any boat-owning," according to Pete Culler, a well-known New England builder of small boats, "is to have a craft to suit your means, and if she has to be small and simple, she's usually more satisfactory than a boat that's a strain to own."

The only really troublesome aspect of owning the Dovekie was owning the trailer. If *Fiddler* was nearly a prototype, being hull number 3, the trailer was Edey and Duff's only venture into the trailer-building business. Heavy and oversized, it was subject to all kinds of problems, and after replacing axles, bearings, wheels, and other assorted parts, I finally, after three years, sold the beast to a farmer for fifty dollars and bought a roller-equipped, lighter, galvanized Cox trailer specifically configured for the Dovekie.

I did make a number of changes to *Fiddler*, encapsulating the lee-boards in epoxy and making solid sliding covers for the two hatch openings. I eventually stripped all the varnish off the wooden parts of the boat and painted everything white. The boat looked sleeker, and the paint reduced maintenance: I changed my appraisal from "weird-looking" to a somewhat hedged "handsome." I installed a small centerboard in the bow which helped *Fiddler* track when going to windward in shallow waters. I made floorboards out of some thin spruce, and made insect screens for the hatch openings. A sailmaker stitched up a tent after my design which converted the cockpit into a "back porch." I fabricated a lazaret cover that hid the gas tank and other unsightly paraphernalia. And when the fifteen-year-old sail had to be replaced, I opted for a Harding sail, just like the original but tanbark in color, a reddish brown that was easier on the eyes.

Maurice Griffiths, writing in *Dream Ships,* reminded me that "it must be kept in mind that so many fittings aboard modern yachts which we think of as absolutely essential . . . were not known a hundred years ago. Our civilized comforts can indeed be analyzed and dropped one by one. . . . It is not necessary, therefore, that a dream ship should be a miniature home of luxury, should boast every shore comfort or should contain every mechanical gadget science and salesmen have brought to our notice for our amusement."

    I have now owned *Fiddler* for more than seven years, and it would be hard to overstate the pleasure that these six hundred pounds of fiberglass have given Evelyn and me. We sometimes talk of shipping it across the Gulf Stream to the Bahamas, or trailering it to the Sea of Cortez. But for the most part the boat is used around the Chesapeake, more often than not on one of the bay's rivers.

THE RIVERS

Tell me how many ever with such small meanes . . . did ever discover so many fayre and navigable Rivers.

—John Smith, *Generall Historie,* 1624

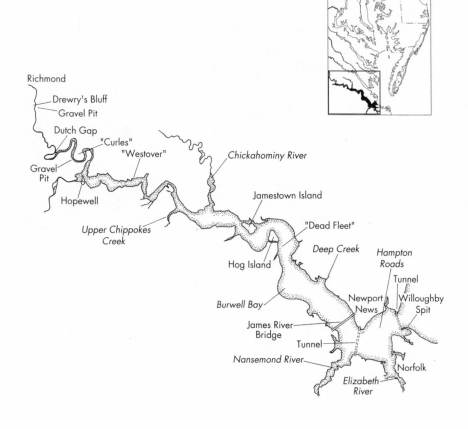

Richmond

Drewry's Bluff
Gravel Pit
Dutch Gap
"Curles"
"Westover"
Gravel
Pit
Hopewell
Chickahominy River

Upper Chippokes
Creek
Jamestown Island
"Dead Fleet"
Deep Creek
Hampton
Roads
Hog Island
Tunnel
Burwell Bay
Newport
News
Willoughby
Spit
James River
Bridge
Tunnel
Nansemond River
Norfolk
Elizabeth
River

The James

This river which we have discovered is one of the famousest Rivers that ever was found by any christian, it ebbes and flowes a hundred and three score miles where ships of great burthen may harbor in safetie.

—George Percy, *Observations,* 1607

Willoughby Spit is just that: a sandy spit of land that helps enclose Hampton Roads and separates it from the Chesapeake Bay. The sand is hardly visible anymore, except on the narrow beaches on the bay side. The spit is dominated by several huge marinas and is the site of the approach lanes to the Hampton Roads Tunnel, which dives—once past Fort Wool, an artificial island at the edge of the Roads entrance—into water more than a hundred feet deep, to emerge at the north end of the entrance at Old Point Comfort.

The entrance to the Roads, and the way to the James, is only three-quarters of a mile wide, and its waters are almost continuously disturbed by an astonishing variety of watercraft: Hampton Roads, with its wharves and anchorages at Norfolk, Newport News, Portsmouth, and Hampton, is one of the world's great natural harbors and one of the busiest ports on the east coast of the United States. It is the world's largest coal port, home to one of America's largest shipbuilding companies, and home base for the U.S. Navy's Atlantic Fleet, as well as a yachting center rivaling Annapolis, and a terminus of the Atlantic Intracoastal Waterway.

Old Point Comfort was named on April 28, 1607, two days after the colonists of the Virginia Company entered the "Bay of Chesupioc," as George Percy related: "Wee rowed over to a point of Land, where wee found a channell, and sounded six, eight, ten, or twelve fathom: which put us in good comfort. Therefore wee named that point of Land,

Cape Comfort." The shoal at the southern end of the channel became a dumping site for ship's ballast, and when the first fort was constructed here, Fort Calhoun, it was locally called Ripraps, after riprap, a foundation made of broken stone thrown together in shallow water or on a soft bottom. Robert E. Lee helped build this fort in 1834; ironically, during the Civil War, Confederate prisoners were confined there. After the war, the fort was renamed Fort Wool, after the Union general John Ellis Wool, who captured Norfolk in the early part of the conflict.

Hampton Roads gives little comfort to a small boat, especially in a fog or drizzle. But here the James begins, or rather, ends. And on Willoughby Spit, overlooking little Willoughby Bay, were several commodious and convenient boat ramps where I proposed to launch *Fiddler*. The ramps—the scene of hectic and confused activity on fair-weather weekends—were deserted on this Thursday afternoon in late May, after days of rain and drizzle. Several cars and pickups were parked next to the ramps, but no boats or trailers were in evidence. Boat ramps and small airfields seem to attract people who gaze wistfully at the little planes in the sky, or the little boats in the water, dreaming, no doubt, of escape and adventure.

As Evelyn expertly backed the trailer to the water's edge, a pale and pudgy man got out of his car and walked over to my Dovekie. A Dovekie invites a lot of attention from sailors and landlubbers alike. It is a strange-looking craft, especially when seated on a trailer before the covers have been removed. There are the usual questions: "What are those things for?" (the questioner points at the leeboards), "How fast will that thing go?" and sometimes "Did you build it yourself?"—on the assumption that anything so weird looking could not have been made by sane, American, *corporate* boatbuilders.

My preparations and provisions must have looked serious enough to indicate that more than a daysail was being contemplated, and my inquisitor dispensed with the preliminaries and barged right in.

"Where are you headed?" he asked.

"Up the James. To Richmond."

"Richmond? You can't do that. All those rapids."

"Rapids?" I asked in astonishment.

"Yes, rapids," he said in a condescending tone. "Once you get to Hopewell, you get rapids. You'll never make it to Richmond."

This was news to me. I knew that President Lincoln had made the trip up the river to Richmond at the end of the Civil War, although the last few miles had to be made on a shallow-draft barge. Maybe I wouldn't make it to Richmond, I thought, but it wouldn't be because of faulty notions of geography. Evelyn, who had continued helping me with the preparations, winked at me. "The boat only weighs six hundred pounds," she whispered. "I'll meet you in Hopewell with the car and help you portage."

"Richmond has a port authority," I insisted. "Tugs and barges go up there all the time. It's less than a hundred miles from here."

"Well, see for yourself," he said angrily, his nautical knowledge having been questioned and found wanting. He returned to his car and roared off.

I put the drain plug in the hull, Evelyn backed the trailer further into the water, and *Fiddler* slid silently into Hampton Roads. The drizzle had stopped a few hours earlier. The sky had begun to clear, and the boat was beginning to dry out. I raised the mast, unfurled the sail, hooked the clew to the sprit, tightened the snotter, and with a push from Evelyn was clear of the dock on the slightest of breezes. "Call me when you get to the rapids," she called.

The James River rises in the Allegheny Mountains, at a place called Iron Gate, near Clifton Forge. It is, along with its sources, wholly within one state, the Commonwealth of Virginia. Its headwaters, the Bullpasture and the Calfpasture, join here to become the Cowpasture, and then the James, which begins to meander nearly three hundred nautical miles toward Hampton Roads, where the James officially ends between Newport News Point and Pig Point. Along the way, in Richmond, seventy-eight miles above the mouth, the river becomes tidal, but it remains fresh to the mouth of Upper Chippokes Creek, halfway between Richmond and Newport News.

The James has had a number of names. When the English settlers arrived in 1607, they reported, "Wee set up a Crosse at the head of this River, naming it Kings River, where we proclaimed James King of England to have the most right unto it." No matter that the river already had a name: Powhatan, after the Indian chief who ruled the twenty-odd tribes along its shores.

It wasn't long, however, before the Kings River became the James River; and before a hundred years had passed the name Powhatan would be forgotten, and the few thousand Indians who had inhabited the river's shores would be dead, diseased, or displaced.

The breeze was still reluctant, but there was just enough of it, out of the north, to propel *Fiddler* across Willoughby Bay toward Sewells Point. Sewells Point is the northernmost part of the gigantic Norfolk Naval Base and Naval Air Station; and every few minutes a helicopter, making a furious noise one hundred feet or so above me on its downwind approach, would drown out the slapping noises of the water against the hull. Actually, the helicopters were higher than one hundred feet, for I never saw the waters ruffled by the rotary wing wash, a turbulence that would surely have capsized us. When there was a break in the noise of the aircraft coming and going I could hear the buzz from the traffic on Interstate 64 which was emerging from the tunnel adjoining the boat ramps.

As I moved further away from shore toward the open waters of Hampton Roads the noise diminished, but the wind increased. I had about five hours of daylight left, but I abandoned my first choice of an anchorage, the little Hampton River, and its snug Sunset Creek. I hadn't gotten my sea legs yet, and the idea of beating across the Roads, with my destination dead to windward, on my first day out seemed to have very little merit. A southwesterly course would give me a pleasant reach and carry me toward Newport News and the waters of the James.

Once out in Hampton Roads, *Fiddler* went from being the only boat on the water to dodging *two* aircraft carriers, one submarine, and a tug and barge, all moving slowly, but not as slowly as I would have liked. I might have had the right of way, being under sail, but testing the thesis would have been suicidal. Actually, the right-of-way issue did take into account the "ability of a vessel constrained by her draft, to maneuver." Small-boat sailors have always known that the real rule is that the biggest vessel has the right of way.

Constraint of draft was a little-known factor in the outcome of the seminal battle that took place just a mile or so west, near Newport News Point, in the spring of 1862 and came to be known as the Battle between the *Monitor* and the *Merrimack*. More accurately, the battle was between the C.S.S. *Virginia* and the U.S.S. *Monitor.*

The U.S.S. *Merrimack* had been burned and abandoned, on purpose, by its own navy the previous year. The Confederates, after capturing the Norfolk Navy Yard on the Elizabeth River, raised and rebuilt the vessel and renamed it the C.S.S. *Virginia.* Covered with four-inch-thick iron plates, she drew twenty-three feet. On March 8, 1862, she cautiously made her way, with a local pilot on board, toward the deeper waters of Hampton Roads, hoping to break the Union blockade of the James. There ensued what came to be known as the Battle of Hampton Roads. Although under heavy fire from both Union ships and shore batteries, the C.S.S. *Virginia* rammed and sank a sloop-of-war, the U.S.S. *Cumberland,* that was lying at anchor at Newport News Point. Then, with two Confederate gunboats accompanying her, she chased the frigate U.S.S. *Congress,* which ran aground and was forced to surrender. The *Virginia*'s commanding officer, Franklin Buchanan, destroyed the *Congress* with red-hot shot. Although Buchanan then tried to attack several other Union ships, the rapidly falling tide forced him to return to Norfolk. But his foray had been an outstanding success for the Confederacy: two Union ships destroyed, and 250 Union sailors killed or wounded. The Confederates had only lost twenty men. Although the ship was not damaged, Buchanan had been wounded by a musket ball, seriously enough so that the next day the *Virginia* was under the command of Lieutenant Catesby Jones. On the rising tide the next morning, Jones returned to Hampton Roads to complete the devastation of the previous day. But midway between Newport News Point and Fort Monroe, where Hampton Roads is deepest, Jones was met by the U.S.S. *Monitor,* under the command of Lieutenant John Worden. The *Monitor* had arrived late the night before, after nearly being sunk in heavy seas on her way south from Long Island. The ship was only five weeks old, having been launched early in February after a record one-hundred-day construction period. It was just in time. The ensuing battle lasted nearly four hours and was fought to a draw. By noon, the falling tide again forced the return of the *Virginia* to Norfolk's Elizabeth River. No lives were lost this time, and the Union blockade remained unbroken. But this battle, in which neither side could gain a victory, forever changed the nature of naval battles. Soon iron men would no longer serve on wooden ships.

The battle was not renewed: each side was afraid to risk its only ironclad. When the Confederates had to abandon Norfolk, the *Virginia,* unable because of her draft to go up the James to Richmond, was destroyed. Now the *Monitor* could make its way safely to Richmond. We will meet her again briefly further up the river at Drewry's Bluff, six miles from Richmond.

Well, *Fiddler* was not constrained by her draft! I made my way across Norfolk Harbor Reach, the deep ship channel, toward the Craney Island Flats, where my chart showed depths of eight and ten feet — there I would be safe from the huge carriers, if not, perhaps, from the tugs and barges. *Fiddler* looked decidedly out of place in the harbor. Here was a little, strange-looking boat with a tanbark sail, dancing across the waves, surrounded by ships, wharves, and cranes, with helicopters and Airborne Warning and Control System (AWACS) planes overhead, sailing toward the Newport News Middle Ground lighthouse and the lowering sun, looking for peace and quiet on the James River.

One of the things that happen if you are not constrained by your draft is that your navigational skills atrophy. After all, you can go where you damn well please. I did, of course, have charts of the James, but some of them, borrowed, or donated by friends, were as old as my Dovekie—dating from 1978. And the imaginary line between Pig Point and Newport News Point which marks the official beginning of the James River was becoming a solid wall on the horizon. My old chart gave no inkling that any obstruction existed. But as I sailed closer it dawned on me that another bridge-tunnel had been built. This one, I was to learn later, was the misnamed Monitor and Merrimac Bridge-Tunnel.

As do all the rivers on the western shore, the James trends toward the northwest—the direction from which the wind was blowing, a little harder now, as a new weather system was settling in over tidewater Virginia. Sailing to windward is something I've always tried to avoid, but there seemed to be few alternatives available to me. If I wanted to get into the river I would have to sail through the opening between the trestle bridges, the half mile or so where the tunnel was located. I could also run back past the Newport News waterfront and look for shelter there, thus losing some hard-won ground. I could bear off toward the south and sail under the bridge where one of the trestles was decidedly higher than the others. But I had no idea what the vertical clearance was, and could hardly experiment to find out whether *Fiddler* could clear or not. I was now nearly upon the serious and somber-looking caisson lighthouse at Newport News Middle Ground, some fifty feet high and half that in diameter, one hundred years old. What I had forgotten was that the foghorn sounded, except in summer, twenty-four hours a day. I should have heard the blasts earlier, but hadn't, and the sudden long, low blast scared the hell out of me. My concentration shattered: in a puff the mainsheet fouled around the rudder, and I had to let it go in order to free it. After a while I managed to re-rig it.

I had now been under way for about two hours, and if my adventures so far were any indication, this was going to be quite a trip. The sun was trying now, but the skies were still gray, the water was gray, and the airplanes and ships were gray. The water had become rougher in the vicinity of the bridge, undoubtedly exacerbated by the changing current, now opposing the wind; and anchoring was out of the question: the water was too choppy and too deep, and the location was too unprotected, with areas on the chart marked "Anchorage for Explosives," "Restricted Anchorage," and "Forbidden Anchorage." Still thinking about sailing under the bridge, I tried to imagine, from a distance, how high, say, four people standing on top of each other would be. I needed twenty-three or twenty-four feet to clear the bridge, but a miscalculation might be fatal. It was too difficult to judge, and in this rough and tumbled water I would be afraid to lower the mast, for fear of losing my—and then its—balance. As I skirted the edge of the bridge-tunnel, a trucker driving a Miller Lite beer truck blasted a greeting my way on his horn. I waved back enthusiastically. But I was beginning now to worry about shelter for the night. And I wasn't even in the James yet.

The sun was fully out of the clouds now, backlighting the waves and emphasizing their height. I spotted a little wrinkle on the chart a half mile east of Pig Point where the bridge straddled the entrance to the James. "Streeter Creek," it was labeled, and the depths at its entrance were given as one foot and one-half foot: the surest way to shipwreck in almost any other vessel, but *Fiddler's* shallow draft was one of the reasons I had become so intrigued with my boat. I turned the rudder and headed for the tiny opening in the marshy shore. With the wind now behind me, and the boards up, I could run *Fiddler* up on the marsh if I had to. The rudder would kick up and out of the way the moment it hit anything. Anxiously peering ahead, trying to look into the black water and tell the future, I braced myself for the inevitable thud. It never came. Suddenly I was in the narrow opening of the creek, perhaps twenty feet wide. Two boat lengths into the creek I made a right turn into its first meander, came head to wind, and got the anchor down in what I guessed was six feet of water, smooth as glass. *Fiddler* sat motionless between the marsh banks. Across the marsh, not a hundred feet away, the water, not quite the James River, was sloshing and hurling its waves against the land. A woods fortuitously hid the span of the bridge. In the other direction, there was a small house and a dock (but no boat). From this distance I could see a child opening the front door and staring out over the marsh. I couldn't tell whether it was a boy or a girl, or make out any facial expression. But I knew what I would do if somebody sailed into my harbor on an evening like this: I'd smile.

It was too early in the year, and too cool, to worry about insects, even though I was surrounded by marshes. Although I was completely sheltered from the waves, the low spartina grass allowed the wind to blow across the boat as she sat to the current, her bow pointing toward the house so as to give me privacy, though I had not seen anybody but the child since my arrival. After a simple dinner, I zipped the spray hood to the gallows, draped the tent cover loosely to the bottom, and slept snugly in my sleeping bag wedged between the storage bins under *Fiddler*'s deck. If the anchor had dragged during the night I would not have known it.

Morning came cool and clear, and after breakfast I raised sail and anchor. There is a tide in the affairs of men which, taken at the ebb, allowed me to sail, but just barely, out of my sheltered anchorage, close-hauled, into the body of water that was not yet the James River. Nothing had changed since I sailed in. Well, not exactly. The sun was behind me now, the traffic on the bridge-tunnel was not moving, and the waves were a little higher. The opening through the bridge-tunnel still lay two miles dead to windward, a very unpleasant prospect. Once under the bridge I could fall off a bit and not have to bash my brains out beating into the wind. Time to take the mast down, a very quick and simple procedure in a Dovekie, but potentially hazardous in this sea. So I ran back into the creek, this time with much more confidence than I had before. Once again in quiet waters, I lowered the mast, briefly considered rowing out again and under the bridge, surely a more seamanlike thing to do, and quickly discarded the option as difficult, exhausting, or even impossible. If gentlemen do not sail to windward, why should they row? As always, the water-jet engine started on the first pull of the starter cord and, throwing out an impressive waterspout, started *Fiddler* moving slowly. As the boat began to gather speed, the stern squatted just enough to submerge the jet nozzle; at full speed, five or six knots in smooth water, the only evidence of an engine would be the turbulence below the surface behind the rudder. And the noise, of course. There was definite motivation to use the engine as little as possible, and as soon as I had cleared the bridge-tunnel I shut the monster down. In much smoother water now, I raised the mast again, and we were off sailing. Though I was traveling alone, I was beginning to think of *Fiddler* and myself as a couple.

The traffic on the bridge was still stalled, but I wasn't making too much progress either, for the current was still against us. Still, I had made it into the James. Pig Point, before the James River Bridge was built five miles upstream in the 1930s, had been the site of the ferry to Newport News. There were still some abandoned piers jutting out into the river, but the point now was the site of a number of truck terminals and industrial parks, and was studded with water towers. Shortly after the bridge was built, the 1937 *Coast Pilot* ruefully noted in a section on the James that "many wharves are in ruins and neglected due to shipments now being made by auto truck." *Plus ça change . . .*

I made my way across the mouth of the Nansemond River, past Barrel Point and the entrance to Chuckatuck Creek, into Batten Bay, where, near some high clumps the chart called Candy Island, I had to tack in order to make my way across the river toward Newport News. The wind was down a bit, to maybe twelve knots, and that, and the sun, helped warm things up. I guessed that the low the night before had been around fifty degrees, and it felt as if it would barely get into the sixties. I wrote "gloves" next to "comb" on the list of items I had forgotten.

This southern shore of the river, flat, rural, and green, was in marked contrast to the opposite shore, where the huge complex and miles of waterfront of the Newport News Shipbuilding and Drydock Company, gray and grimy, its cranes and derricks reaching hundreds of feet into the sky, completely dominated the skyline. I waved to a crabber working his pots in the shallow waters off Ragged Island, and headed for the deeper water that had lured shipbuilders to Newport News.

Newport News was spelled Newport Ness on several old maps. *Ness* is an Old English word meaning "promontory," or "point," and has nothing to do with news. As for the other part of the name: Captain John Smith looms so large in the early history of Virginia that it is often forgotten that the 1607 expedition was under the command of Captain Christopher Newport.

Newport News Shipbuilding and Drydock Company is the largest, and oldest, privately owned shipyard in the nation. With thirty thousand workers, it is also the largest private employer in Virginia. Its founder, Collis Potter Huntington, had insisted, "We shall build good ships here at a profit—if we can—at a loss—if we must—but always good ships." Some of those good ships, in various stages of construction, now loomed ahead, but didn't seem to be getting closer very fast. It was now nearly noon. The wind had dropped to less than five knots, and the current still wasn't doing me any favors either. As I made my way up the river, the current would stay against me longer. I figured that it would be late afternoon, and another five or ten miles upstream, before the tide would favor me. And by then I would hope to be anchored somewhere in bucolic bliss. Still, there was lunch to contend with. It seemed the wrong place to just sit and drift while I made a sandwich, and the forty-, fifty-, and sixty-foot depths made it difficult to anchor.

As I inched my way toward shore, just south of the shipyard, between a submarine in drydock and some tugboats resting between chores, I saw a tiny little strip of sand: a beach in downtown Newport News! The indentation looked inviting, a great place to beach *Fiddler* and have a picnic lunch. But as I slowly approached for a closer inspection, the inviting beach turned out to be an illusion. The sand was strewn with broken glass, jagged pieces of metal, and shattered concrete blocks. "If it looks too good to be true," some wag once said, "it probably is." At the last minute, I bore off and headed back toward the river. Blanketed by the large vessels and pushed around by the current, I had all I could do to avoid the tugs. I was beginning to think about rowing again when a loud blast ended my deliberation. For one moment I thought I was being run down by a supertanker. Then, as I located the source of the noise, I noticed the welding sparks dry up, and the pipefitters and sand-blasters stopped fitting and blasting. It was high noon, and lunchtime on the waterfront. This made me even hungrier. A few hundred yards offshore I left *Fiddler* to her own devices. In any other boat this would have been called heaving-to, but with *Fiddler* it was different. With so little wind, she was hardly going anywhere, the current checking any forward progress. The shipyard's security launch kept eyeing us suspiciously. Twenty minutes and a tuna fish sandwich later we were on our way again.

Negotiating the James River Bridge was not especially enrapturing. I did have a chart that showed this bridge's particulars. There were two openings: the main lift bridge, which offered a fifty-foot vertical clearance when closed, and a smaller, fixed span a mile or so further west, with a clearance of twenty-two feet — exactly what *Fiddler* needed, but too close for comfort. I chose the main span, naturally, and it was a good thing that the bridge did not need to lift for me, because the ensuing delay in my getting through it would have caused pandemonium and wreaked havoc on Newport News's traffic. With little wind and an adverse current, it took me nearly a quarter of an hour to safely clear the bridge. At first it was a challenge. Then it became a point of honor. It ended with plain stubbornness.

Clear of the bridge, in freer air, I had plenty of time to think about possible anchorages, two of which were virtually in sight on the horizon. The Pagan River, a small tributary that meanders toward Smithfield, would give me a better slant on what little wind there was, but I would probably lose my advantage fighting the current. Deep Creek, beyond Blunt Point, near the entrance of the Warwick River, was a little closer, and its current might not be as strong. I opted to delay the decision for an hour or two and headed directly between my two possible destinations, toward the remains of White Shoal lighthouse.

When I had last visited here, two decades earlier, it was to make some photographs for a book that was later published as *The Lighthouses of the Chesapeake*. At that time the structure was still recognizably a lighthouse, although long abandoned and in decrepit condition. Its board-and-batten privy still hung from one of its walls, suspended over the water. Appropriately enough, what was left now on top of the old screw pile foundation was a few boards, part of the old floor, and a tremendous heap of guano on the side where the old outhouse had been. The birds had taken over. Dozens of gulls were excitedly circling the structure as I silently approached. The lighthouse had been built in 1855, and was described in the 1869 annual report of the Lighthouse Board as being "of the oldest and most inferior design." Inferior or not, it was still standing, sort of, nearly a century and a half later.

The Pagan River was now a little closer than Deep Creek. Both were about four miles away, but the latter lay due north, closer to my goal. Deep Creek it would be. And I would row to Deep Creek. I did have other options: using the engine, or anchoring and waiting for a breeze. But I used the jet-pump engine so little, and was so reluctant to use it, that I had not bothered to check how much fuel I had—until now. It looked to be about a pint: maybe ten minutes' worth. As for anchoring, and waiting: I think that I was too eager to move on; it was too early in the voyage, and I had not yet settled down to the rhythm that cruising requires. At least for now, there had to be a destination, an attainable one. Later in my cruises I found it easy to be patient, to wait for wind or tide, but that was not yet the case.

I decided to save my pint of fuel and row as far as I could. I removed the rowing-port covers, put the thwart between the storage bins, retrieved the two ten-foot oars from under the deck, and looking for all the world like a Greek galley, started toward Blunt Point. *Fiddler* is a decent rowing boat. With the mast down and the boards up, I could, in a flat calm, probably do better than two knots. Two hours to Deep Creek. But the current had not yet abated, and I was probably making good only about a mile and a half over the bottom. Facing aft, I could still see, almost five hours later, the drydocks and cranes of the Newport News shipyard. Closer to shore the current was weaker, but progress was still painfully slow. It was easy to sympathize with earlier mariners, frustrated by their total dependence on wind and tides, or on oar power.

Thus far, on my first full day on the James River, I had seen one sailboat, two motorboats, two small tugs, and one floating crane. And the suspicious security launch at lunchtime. Even a hundred years ago, with *leisure time* an unknown term, there had been a lot more traffic on any stretch of the river, and not all of it commercial.

The houses along the river were large, some even beautiful, with lawns stretching down to the river. Ahead, flanking the Warwick River, was Mulberry Island. I could make out its southern tip, Lands End. It was a lovely sight. Surely the Virginia Company settlers must have considered this place before Jamestown.

A small motorboat caught up with me, and I was almost tempted to ask for a tow. But even if I had raised my thumb, the occupants would not have noticed. They were going ten or twenty times as fast as I was, and they were oblivious. Earlier in the day I had cursed a motorboat that threw a huge wake my way, and now I was thinking about hitching a ride. How ironic. An hour and a half later I had rowed as far as the entrance to the Warwick River, and I needed a break. The motor was enlisted to help out for the last mile, but in a few minutes, at the narrow opening to Deep Creek, it burped, and quit. (I found out the next morning that there was still a bit of gas left, but the air vent to the gas tank had vibrated shut.) The oars went back in the water, and *Fiddler* silently negotiated the rest of the channel into the harbor at Deep Creek.

There are dozens of Deep Creeks scattered around the Chesapeake Bay, and all of them are shallow. I didn't stick to the channel, and at some point I heard and felt the rudder kick up, but under oar power the rudder wasn't necessary anyway.

"Can I buy some gas here?" I called from my rowing position—with only my head visible above the deck of the boat—to two little boys fishing at the edge of the harbor. Two astonished faces nodded simultaneously. Drifting closer to the little marina and its gas dock, I had to scull the last few yards to come alongside a crabbing boat tied to the rickety wharf. A sign on the front door said, "CLOSED, but Smile, You're on Video." I ambled back to my boat. There was another marina, or perhaps a yacht club, further up the creek, but I'd had enough exercise for one day. I sculled across the channel to the shallowest and quietest part of the harbor, anchored, and began my evening culinary exercise on my two-burner propane stove: chicken, rice, and squash, the chicken from a can, the rice from a bag, and the squash from Evelyn's garden. I managed to wash up using less than two quarts of the three gallons of fresh water I carried.

Near sunset I was deluged, suddenly and simultaneously, with a host of visitors in two inflatable dinghies from two cruising catamarans anchored at the other side of the harbor. They approached cautiously in the shallow water. They were David and Gail Bridges and Garland and Anne Gray, and their children, and they wanted to talk about Dovekies and shoal-draft boats.

"We saw you rowing out there earlier today. Hell of a current," Garland said. "We were out there too, but we finally gave up and motored in." The Bridges and Grays were inveterate weekend cruisers and loved exploring the James in their shallow-draft multihulls. But they had never been above Hopewell. I explained my river exploration plans and my intention to write about the journeys.

"You'd like a book I have that sounds sort of like that. It's called *Western Wind, Eastern Shore*. Have you heard of it?" David asked. I said I had, and introduced myself as its author. At sunset, and the children's bedtime, I was invited to tour the multihulls. After another hour's talk aboard the Gray's Eder catamaran, Garland ran me back to *Fiddler* in her serene anchorage. The sleeping bag was inviting on this chilly, starry evening. I had no blisters, but I was aware of possessing certain muscles

I hadn't known I had before. I had sailed, rowed, motored, and sculled my little boat, all in one day, and I couldn't remember having done *that* before.

Morning was like the day before: cool and clear. A great blue heron was fishing for breakfast in a few inches of water a boat length away. When I stood up to stretch my legs and brush my teeth, it languidly took off, as always into the wind, this morning into the northwest. The tide was out, but the water was deep enough for *Fiddler* to float. The marina would open at eight. The earlier I got started, the longer I would have the current in my favor.

Fiddler carried only one anchor, surely an irresponsible notion in any cruising boat worthy of the name. It was an eight-pound Bruce, an anchor first developed for holding North Sea oil rigs in place. Unlike most other anchors, it has no movable parts, and it had always held the first time I set it. Sometimes, of course, it was possible to walk the anchor out and set it by hand. Another reason that the Bruce never failed may have been that I usually gave the anchor plenty of scope. Scope is the relationship between the depth of the water and the amount of rope paid out. Seven to one is considered optimal, but in my Dovekie I could sometimes have the proper scope with only six or seven feet of anchor line out. It never took long to recover the anchor.

I sculled to the marina and bought a few gallons of gas from the sleepy-looking attendant, who was watching the Saturday morning cartoons on television.

"Anything else?" he asked.

"Where can I buy a comb?" I asked. He stared at my hair.

"The country store across the road might have one." I looked down the road toward the Menchville Country Store but saw no sign of commerce.

"What time do they open?"

"Well, they're kind of independent, it might be nine or ten, hard to tell. Have some coffee."

"Thanks, but I need to catch the current upriver. I'm headed for Richmond."

"Richmond?" He was rummaging now through his desk drawers, perhaps looking for a comb. He looked at my hair again.

"I've never been there. By water." He looked a little unbelieving but didn't say anything about rapids at Hopewell. He didn't find what he was looking for in the drawer.

"Well, it's a nice day for it," he said, and went back to the adventures of the Flintstones.

I was able to sail out of Deep Creek on a fine fifteen-knot northwesterly breeze. Sweater weather. A lone crabber was baiting his pots in the Warwick River. When I cleared Jail Point, the marshy tip of Mulberry Island, I was back in the James, here at its widest, in the part of the river called Burwell Bay—"a fine sheet of water," as *The James River Tourist,* a steamboat company booklet, proclaimed at the turn of the century. The river channel here now skirts the edge of Burwell Bay, but river traffic used to have to skirt Point of Shoals, a few miles to the west. In 1837 a lighthouse service representative, while searching for eligible sites for new lights, suggested that three lighthouses be built in the James River but that "if it be intended to erect one light, and *only one,* then I would, in that case, recommend its being placed on the Point of Shoals, as it is the most dangerous situation on James River." A lighthouse was built there, but the light was dismantled in the 1950s when the shoaling in Burwell Bay had become so severe that a new channel had to be dredged and the beacon was no longer necessary.

Fiddler disdained the new channel, as we skirted the marshes of Mulberry Island. Then a strange sight loomed five miles ahead, and as I got closer I realized that we were approaching perhaps a hundred ships moored in the middle of the river. Called, variously, "the dead fleet," "the ghost fleet," or "the idle fleet," the anchorage had held as many as 750 craft after World War II but was now down to 119 vessels, mostly cargo ships, held in readiness for emergency use by the armed forces. Surplus grain had been stored in many of the ships during the fifties and early sixties. Most of the old Liberty and Victory class ships were sold for scrap. The old Bay Line flagship *President Warfield,* with a passenger capacity of 540, was part of the fleet after World War II. She was later to become famous as the eponymous vessel in the Leon Uris novel *Exodus.* She was sold, ostensibly for scrap, in November 1946, for $8,028, but was dispatched to Europe with the help of Jewish American philanthropists, and eventually carried 4,554 displaced Jews from France to Israel. She caught fire in Haifa Harbor in 1952, and her remains were once again sold for scrap.

Still, 119 ships anchored in this stretch of the James were an impressive sight, and they nearly blocked the river. Or so it seemed. The official name of this armada is the Maritime Administration James River Reserve Fleet, and a stern note on the chart warns: "No vessels or other watercraft, except those owned or controlled by the U.S. Government, shall cruise or anchor between Reserve Fleet units, within 500 feet of the extreme units of the fleet, unless specific permission to do so has first been granted in each case by the enforcing agency."

I wasn't planning to anchor, but I was certainly cruising between the hulls. It was the only way I could beat my way up the river. When in the lee of the huge ships I hardly made any progress, but when we emerged from their wind shadows, *Fiddler* would be hard pressed, occasionally heeling far enough for water to come trickling in through the gaps around the oar-port covers. It was feast or famine for about ten minutes as I made my way through the fleet. I discovered during one of my tacks through the fleet that one of the vessels—a ship used for lifting heavy machinery, such as locomotives—was called *Marine Fiddler.* I later learned that *Marine Fiddler* was "under house arrest." Peregrine falcons had nested in the ship, and the Endangered Species Act kept her from being moved.

Once I was clear of the anchorage, a more westerly trend of the river gave me a more favorable slant. A lone windsurfer near the distant shore ahead was trying over and over again to stay upright. It was a hard breeze for a beginner, and soon the sailor gave up. I ran the Dovekie up on a little beach in the lee of the high banks in the bight in the river near Kingsmill, and made lunch.

I had now come abreast of Hog Island, a low, marshy peninsula where the Jamestown colonists, after abandoning their settlement in 1610, met the boat that Lord Delaware had sent ahead up the river to inform the settlers that the resupply was on its way. As John Smith related it: "At noone they fell from Jamestown to the isle of hogs, and the next morning to Mulberry Point, at which time they descried Lord Delaware's long boat."

When I rounded Hog Island for that first abrupt turn in the river, the view took my breath away. Three or four miles ahead was an island, or perhaps a peninsula, for across some low marsh I could see water: a further bend in the river. The marsh was Jamestown Island, unexpectedly close.

Ever since that day in May 1607 when the English colonists, all 105 of them, landed on Jamestown Island, scores of writers and scholars have chastised them for picking the wrong spot. The instructions from the Virginia Company were very clear: "When it Shall please God to Send you on the Coast of Virginia you shall Do your best Endeavour to find out a Safe port in the Entrance of Some navigable River making Choise of Such a one as runneth furthest into the Land." They had done that. But there were other provisions: "Neither must You plant in a low and moist place because it will prove unhealthful." It was clear to me, however, sailing up the river on this bright afternoon, how the spot might have looked like Eden. They had, after all, been living on their boats for nearly half a year (although they had stopped at many islands, including the Canaries and several of the Leeward and Windward Islands). Nearly four hundred years later, I wouldn't have hesitated to settle down on this alluring spot on the river. But looks can be deceiving.

"This island," wrote Ann Woodlief in *In River Time: The Way of the James*, "was probably the worst piece of real estate on the river in the summer time, and the Indians knew it. It lay very low, invaded by stagnant swamps, and it had no freshwater springs." But the colonists were thinking about defense, and about the ease of unloading their ships, for on the edge of the island the river's current had carved deep channels, where, as George Percy related, "our shippes doe lie so neere the shoare that they are moored to the Trees in six fathom water."

A lot of shoaling and a lot of erosion had taken place during these hundreds of years. Jamestown Island, one mile wide and a couple of miles long, is separated from the mainland by a little creek called Back River and by a shallow estuary called the Thorofare. Probably, except for their depths, they have changed little. The trees were undoubtedly bigger and the waters clearer in the 1600s. But except for the twelve-story-tall cooling towers of the power station three miles across the river, nothing seemed to have changed.

A letter attributed to Edward Maria Wingfield (the first president of the first council of the first English colony in America) stated in June 1607: "We are sett down 80 miles within a River, for breadth, sweetnes of water, length navigable upp into the contry deepe and bold Channell so stored with Sturgion and other sweete Fish as no mans fortune hath ever possessed the like." The "sweetnes of water," however, was a delusion. In the summer this stretch of the river lay in a zone of maximum turbidity, as scientists call it, where fresh and salt water mix but little real movement of water takes place, an ideal environment for the introduction of dysentery and typhoid, and possibly, salt poisoning. In an intriguing essay that reads like a detective story, the historian Carville V. Earle makes a solid case that the catastrophic mortality rates in Jamestown were caused by drinking the water of the river.

The colonists have been much maligned for their laziness and apathy. "Never was there a set of men worse adapted for the sober business of establishing a colony," wrote one scholar. George Percy, the colony's first chronicler, wrote: "Our drinke [was] cold water taken out of the River, which was at a floud verie salt, at low tide full of slime and filth, which was the destruction of many of our men." That, as Earle explains, was the cause of the lazy and factious behavior, classic symptoms of salt poisoning.

Off Black Point, the eastern tip of Jamestown Island, I nearly capsized *Fiddler*. As I approached the island, I was preoccupied with trying to imagine the feelings of the colonists. The sight was pretty now; it must have been beautiful then. For some reason, I wanted to calculate how many days had elapsed since the colonists first saw it, and was trying to subtract May 13, 1607, the day Jamestown was first sighted, from May 21, 1993, the date I first saw the island. Just as I came close to the solution, a vicious gust hit my little boat. *Fiddler* heeled as far as she had ever heeled. My daydreaming and arithmetic exercise came to an abrupt halt. The James River was over the top of the oar-port, and despite the fact that the oar-port was closed, water poured in around the edges. I wished I could have taken credit for the recovery, but most of it must go to the boat: as she heeled, the wind spilled out of the sail, and the rudder instantly made her head into the wind. At the same time, I'd let go of the mainsheet, and *Fiddler* was upright again, luffing into the wind. The boat, and the wind, had my total attention. Later, I tried to imagine what would have happened if we had capsized. The boat, of course, wouldn't sink, having been made of foam-core fiberglass. But almost everything I had on board would have floated out or sunk before I could have righted the boat. There had been, I knew, several instances of capsizing with the Dovekie, and according to these reports, righting the boat had been simple. But it would have taken hours to bail her out, the engine would have been soaked in salt water, and it would surely have ruined my afternoon! I vowed to do my arithmetic and daydreaming from now on only in winds of less than ten miles per hour, and only when the wind was aft of the beam.

I figured that Richmond was still about fifty miles ahead, a long way up the James. Even the *Waterway Guide* (a regional guidebook for boaters), ever enthusiastic about traveling by boat, agreed that it was a long way: "Richmond is a center of historic highlights," its author admitted, "but there are easier ways of visiting them than by boat." At least I had the river mostly to myself.

It was only midafternoon when I anchored one hundred feet or so from Jamestown Island, in the protection of the Thorofare and in about three feet of water. I wanted to go around Jamestown, up the Thorofare, through Back River, and back into the James, underneath a twelve-foot-high bridge that kept out many large powerboats and all sailboats. But that could wait till morning. It had started to rain, and I would have to lower the mast to make up my tent anyway, so I settled down early.

A half hour later I had tidied things up and sat, comfortable and dry, in my cockpit tent. I studied the chart to decide how to divide up the fifty miles to my destination. My goal was to make roughly twelve miles a day. That didn't sound like much, given the fact that *Fiddler* was capable of making six knots under the right circumstances. Two hours a day, and bingo! But the right circumstances were not always in ready supply. Often the destination lay to windward, and tacking took time. The wind didn't always blow at a steady fifteen knots. The current was often not fair. There might be lay days, when there was no wind, or too much. I had sailed this day for about six hours, in winds ranging in speed from five to more than fifteen miles per hour, with occasional higher gusts, and I had made good about fifteen miles toward my destination. It wasn't much, but it was more than my quota, and it had been a great day to sail.

There were in late May plenty of daylight hours, close to fifteen. But there were always chores to be done. I might have to clean the boat, cook my meals, plan my navigation, or look for water, fuel, or groceries. I had things to fix and dishes to wash, a log to be kept, hair to be washed, and a book to read, although there never seemed to be much time for that. After dark there was always my small reading light, but by the time it got dark I was usually too tired to read.

It was pleasant, however, to sit in the cockpit after dinner, snug and dry, and watch the island's shore dissolve into the night, as a navigational marker miles to the east, the only evidence of this century, relentlessly flashed red every four seconds.

Sunrise at Jamestown was nothing short of magical. The first rays of the sun struck through the starboard oar-port. I peeked outside, momentarily disoriented by the low perspective, the Lexan-covered oar-ports being only inches above the water. I unzipped the tent, my "back porch," from its frame and felt the warmth of the sun. Little wisps of fog danced on the edges of the Thorofare, then evaporated as I watched. The sky was pale blue and cloudless, and the water without a ripple. A heavy dew covered the boat, except where my tent had been. The woods and marshes around me looked even more pristine in the low, slanting light.

I made coffee, managed to toast bread in the frying pan, and poached my weekly allotment of two eggs. A banana and a glass of orange juice completed the feast. It was amazing what varied meals I could concoct without having access to refrigeration. I washed the dishes in James River water, but, mindful of the health problems of the colonists, I had boiled the water for ten minutes.

There was no need to wait for a breeze, since I had to go under the bridge with my mast down, under either oar power or engine power. Still, I waited for the sun to climb higher and dry my tent material, which I had draped over the mast and sprit. I found myself thinking about a Sunday newspaper, and smiled at the thought. There was hardly a store left on the entire river. There had been more traffic here in the eighteenth and nineteenth centuries than there was now. And having wanted to submerge myself in a world like that of the seventeenth century, why did I now want to know what was going on in the modern world? Old habits. Still, there were the funnies . . .

By eight my canvas had been dried out and stowed. The previous day I had started under sail from an anchor, but this day started with the roar of my infernal combustion engine. I motored for fifteen minutes, against the current, through the ever-narrowing Thorofare, past Pyping Point, into Back River, and under the bridge back into the James, a distance of less than two miles. Except for the little bridge and a couple of duck blinds, there was nothing to remind me of modern life.

I turned northwest, toward Richmond. The big automobile ferry to Scotland, across the river, had just left its pier at Glass House Point, south of which I saw a small basin where there were replicas of the three vessels that had sailed to Jamestown in 1607.

I motored over to the dilapidated pier. Visitors here were not expected to come by water, but I was anxious to go ashore to verify something that had baffled me in my reading about Jamestown. What were the names, the correct names, of these three ships? I assumed that I would be able to read the names on their sterns, their builders surely having done their homework. A lot of writers had not done theirs.

There seemed to have been hardly any difficulty with *Discovery*, the smallest ship. She was of the type known as "pinnace," from the Latin *pinus*, pine tree, source of the timber from which such ships were commonly made. Yet one popular encyclopedia published in the 1940s stated that "pinnace" was the name of the ship! She carried twenty-one people across the Atlantic.

There had been centuries-long confusion, however, about the two other ships. I had seen *God Speed*, and *Goodspeed*; I had read *Susan Constant*, *Sarah Constant*, and even *Susan Comstock*. The author of an obscure book called *Seeing the Sunny South*, clearly befuddled by all this, listed *four* ships making their way to the New World: *Sarah*, *Susan Constant*, *Goodspeed*, and *Discovery*. The *Encyclopedia Americana* decided not to get involved, and mentioned "three frail ships." Such eminent historians as Arthur Pierce Middleton and Philip L. Barbour held opposing views, Middleton opting for *Sarah Constant*, *Goodspeed*, and *Discovery*, while Barbour firmly held to *Susan Constant*, *God Speed*, and *Discovery*.

It turned out that ships in the seventeenth century didn't display their names on their sterns, as a helpful guide explained after the exhibit opened. And the *God Speed*, or *Goodspeed*, was not even at the pier, but being refurbished at a boatyard in Hampton Roads. I then came across the "orders for the Council of Virginia," dated December 10,

1606, in which a scribe unwittingly wrote, "First Whereas the Good Ship Called the Sarah Constant and the Ship Called the Godspeed..." Edward D. Neill, in his *History of the Virginia Company of London,* published in 1869, miscopied "Godspeed" as "Goodspeed," and the error has since persisted.

After all this, I was happy to learn that *Susan Constant, Godspeed,* and *Discovery* were the proper names of those historic vessels. But what about Sarah Constant Park, at Willoughby Spit? Who would tell the lifeguards?

The promised breeze did not arrive. With the water now the color and texture of the sky, and the current hard against me, I decided to motor the few miles to the entrance of the Chickahominy River, where I needed to go under a bridge with a twelve-foot vertical clearance. Well, I didn't really need to, but there was that possibility of picking up a Sunday paper. The Chickahominy River can still be navigated for nearly twenty miles, as far as Walkers Dam. Before the dam was built, the river could be navigated much further, perhaps as much as thirty miles, and it was here that Captain John Smith went several times, in a barge, in November 1607, to trade with the Chickahominy Indians for corn. In December 1607 Smith returned to the river for further exploration, and was taken prisoner and nearly killed. As every child in America learns, however, he was saved by Pocahontas, the daughter of the great Indian chief Powhatan.

At the Powhatan Campground, next to the Ferry Point swing bridge, I was able to find a Sunday paper, fresh water, and a comb. I rowed back out into the James, where more than an hour later I picked up the current. Whatever progress I made that afternoon was courtesy of the current: I gave up on rowing at Dancing Point, but there wasn't enough breeze to speed me beyond the one-knot velocity of the current. It took nearly four hours to go about five miles. On the south side of the river were a small trailer camp and some riverside cabins. A few bigger houses had been built on top of the cliffs, here fifty or sixty feet high.

By late afternoon the current began to slacken, and I nudged *Fiddler* into Upper Chippokes, a shallow creek at the place where the James officially becomes fresh, beyond which a Virginia fishing license is needed before fishermen can become complete anglers. Naturally, when I turned southwest into the creek, a little breeze sprang up . . . out of the southwest. It took nearly an hour to work the boat up the creek to a small cove, but it was a pleasurable time after the stillness of the day. A half mile into the creek I lost sight of Jamestown Island, less than ten miles to the east.

Once anchored in two feet of water in my little cove, surrounded on three sides by cypress trees, and on the fourth by a space empty of people, houses, and boats, I decided to take advantage of this privacy to bathe. The river, though fresh now, was still cold, and bathing in two feet of water wouldn't be easy. I carried a plastic water bag on the stern underneath the tiller. "Hot Water from the Sun," its label promised, and the sun had been shining on its three gallons all day. The bag felt hot enough for comfort—one hundred degrees, at least, I figured. There were two problems with this arrangement. The first was that in order for the shower to work, the bag and its sprayer had to be hoisted to a high place. Since the sail on a Dovekie is rolled up and stored alongside the mast, the halyard, the rope that raises and lowers the sail, was essentially in a permanent position and not easily usable. And the mast, of course, had to be in the upright position. But there was a small hook on the mast about six feet above the deck which I used for securing the furled sail, and I could hang the bag from it. The second problem was more vexing. Since Dovekies have no bilge, any water coming into the boat would cover the floor—and make for a damp night. I therefore had to close the two standing room hatches, the two openings in the deck, and climb on *Fiddler's* deck near the mast step to take my one-gallon "navy shower": wet down, lather up, rinse off. On land, of course, I could have hung the shower bag from a tree, but my anchorage was not rimmed by terra firma. It was an awkward but warm and welcome bath. Some flies showed up in early evening, and I lowered the mast and tented myself in. By nightfall I had finished the paper's crossword puzzle. One of the last words to be filled in had been a six-letter word meaning "showered," and ending in "-ed." It took me a long time to figure it out. It was "rained."

"*The thing you're after / may lie around the bend,*" the poet Charles Olson once wrote. The thing I was after, a favoring breeze, lay around the second sharp turn in the James, around Kennon Marsh, between Bachelor and Sturgeon Points, where the river narrowed to a thousand feet. There was plenty of wind, but in the wind shadow of the marsh, which was rimmed with many trees, I couldn't stem the tide, which was running at full bore. Even with the wind out of the northwest, it was a warm morning, and I had started out — and stayed — in shorts. I could have known, just by looking at the chart, that the current would be strong here. It had scoured the bottom to the deepest depth in the river, ninety-four feet. It took two hours and a half dozen attempts to round the point. Hard on the wind, I would seem to be slicing through the water at a respectable speed, and I would see the trees on the opposite shore sliding backward. By staying, as far as was possible, in the shallower water and the weaker current on the edges, I was eventually able, yard by yard, to clear the point. Yet it was not in any sense discouraging. It was an absurd game that I played with the river, a game that required little skill, but great patience and lots of time.

The stretch of river after Sturgeon Point, half a mile wide and four miles long, trends southwesterly, and I was able to sail with the mainsheet started, the wind now behind me. A mile or so down this reach, opposite the Upper Brandon manor house, a beautiful 1825 building in the Federal neoclassical style, there was a narrow opening, the common mouth of two creeks (Kittewan and Mapsico), which was guarded by a lone bald cypress in the middle of the entrance, from whose trunk grew a huge queen anne's lace plant. I'd been under way for nearly five hours and had made good only five miles toward Richmond. But it was lunchtime, it was an intriguing place to stop, and within a few hours the current would favor me again.

I anchored in six feet of water at the confluence of the two creeks, in the most serene surroundings I had yet seen on the James. And the warmest temperatures I had yet experienced on this cruise. I thought about a swim in this lovely and lonely spot, and rigged the swimming ladder and donned my shorts. This was apparently seen, by hundreds of flies, as a unique opportunity for celebrating the month after which they were named. I decided against a swim. Robert Beverley had written in 1705 that "All the Annoyances and Inconveniences of the Country, may fairly be summed up, under these three Heads, Thunder, Heat, and troublesome Vermin." I draped myself in some towels, but after a short time the pests disappeared.

After lunch *Fiddler* slowly swung on her anchor in the opposite direction: the tide had turned. During the next hour I covered a distance that, at the speed I was traveling earlier in the day, would have taken five hours. Still, it was a struggle, but of a different sort. With the wind both more fluky and more puffy, gusting at times to twenty miles per hour, it took all my concentration to keep my little boat upright. I thought about reefing my sail (that is, reducing its sail area), but it seemed a short distance to the next point, Weyanoke, where I would be sheltered once again, and the wind would no longer be on the nose. The time to reef, as all experienced sailors know, is as soon as you first think of it. Still, knowing that the wind often follows the river's course, and thinking that at the next turn my problem might not go away, I steered *Fiddler* toward the lee of a low cliff and tucked in a reef, a simple, two- or three-minute procedure. The change was remarkable. The boat was much easier to steer, and I felt in control again. And our speed was not affected. Instead of a stressful, adrenaline-pumping strain, the next few hours offered sedate and relaxing sailing. It didn't matter whether I sat on the windward or leeward side. Jibes presented no problems, and beating to windward was actually pleasant.

In the next stretch, near Flowerdew Hundred Plantation, I encountered a large outbound freighter, one of nearly 150 vessels that call in Richmond every year. At the beginning and the end of this stretch, General Ulysses S. Grant, commander of the Union forces during the

Civil War, moved his troops across on his march from Spottsylvania Courthouse to the front at Petersburg. A three-thousand-foot-long pontoon bridge was laid across the river between Wilcox Wharf and Windmill Point, and another spanned the thousand feet from Weyanoke Point to Fort Powhatan. In less than forty-eight hours, 130,000 men and their equipment were marched across.

At the next point, Ducking-Stool, I turned into little Herring Creek, a shallow, marsh-lined waterway behind Westover Plantation. It was booby-trapped with fishnet stakes and nets. At a spot where I could see the river shimmer across the marsh, but where I was still far enough from the marsh, I hoped, to be safe from flying critters, I dropped the hook for the night.

I was only a few dozen miles from Richmond, but my surroundings looked much as they would have to Captain Newport (and John Smith and twenty-two others) when they went "in his shallop to discover up the river" a few days after the disembarkation on Jamestown Island: "They were so ravished with the admirable sweetness of the streame, and with the pleasant land trending along on either side, that their joy exceeded, and with great admiration they praised God."

Later explorers agreed. A letter written by one of the colonists, Peter Winne, in 1608, begins: "I was not so desirous to come into this Country, as I am now willing here to end my dayes: for I finde it a farr more pleasant, and plentifull country than any report made mencion of. upon the River which wee are seated I have gon six or seaven score miles *[sic]*, and so farr is navigable."

So farr, so good. But I was approaching Hopewell, and as my geography mentor on Willoughby Spit had warned, there were those rapids to be reckoned with.

Anxious to catch the last of the flooding current, I was under way at sunrise. But by the time I made my way out of the creek into the James, it was already too late. Still, I would have slack water for a little while, and a nice, steady breeze allowed for progress up the river, past that most beautiful of riverfront plantations, Westover, with its fine Georgian architecture and ancient tulip poplars. The mansion was built in 1730 by William Byrd II, planter, diarist, satirist, and founder of the city of Richmond. Having been born on the James, he seemed fond of rivers (and named Richmond after Richmond on the Thames), but he was not fond of sailors, having once written, "They are commonly men of no aspiring genius, and their understanding rises little higher than Instinct. . . . One may as soon tutor a monkey to speak or a French woman to hold her tongue as to bring a Skipper to higher Flights of Reason." He was buried in the center of the walled garden, a few feet from the river.

Past Westover was Berkeley Plantation, its main house not visible from the river, and its waterfront disfigured by a huge, crude, plywood billboard made to look like a colonial sailing vessel. General McClellan headquartered 140,000 Union troops on the extensive property for two months in 1862. Here the river widened again into a bowl-shaped body called Tar Bay.

Hopewell, known until well after the Civil War as City Point, was still a half dozen miles to the west, but it had already made its presence known — visually and olfactorily. Despite the steady breeze, my progress was slowing. The full ebbing current, running at perhaps two knots, would be keeping Hopewell in sight longer than I wanted it to.

Near the Benjamin Harrison Bridge, a lift bridge at Jordan Point named after a signer of the Declaration of Independence who was a three-time governor of Virginia, I spotted some sailboat masts. Soon the Jordan Point Yacht Haven came into view. Near its buoyed entrance I rolled up my sail, and then motored to the fuel dock. I counted seven sailboats and guessed that there were a hundred powerboats. I felt ridiculous buying exactly one gallon of gas — all I could squeeze into the little tank. When I went inside to pay the $1.36 bill I had incurred, I saw a sign behind the counter: "It's Not Company Policy, It's Just the Way We Do Things around Here." The way they did things around there was to allow me, as a *paying* customer, to take a shower in their spiffy bathroom. What bliss! Still, not wanting to get used to this abundance of water, I took a very short shower, so short that the marina manager noticed. "I know exactly how you feel," he said. "Guilty. I know—I used to live on a boat."

Just before noon I was off again, with the current now helping to speed me around Hopewell as quickly as possible. I also tried to take a shortcut by following the shore around Eppes Island. The chart showed mostly one-foot depths, enough for *Fiddler*. But it also showed a bewildering variety of other notations: "Snags" and "Subm Piles," "Stakes," "Spoil Area," and "Obstr," not to mention at least a half dozen wreck symbols. It was dead low tide, and my plan didn't work. Amid the wrecks of old sunken ships and barges *Fiddler* finally grounded out. Four inches was too much draft. I chose not to wait for the tide to float her. Instead, I stepped out of the boat, making her 170 pounds lighter and thereby floating her a fraction of an inch higher—enough so I could walk her off the flats. I pointed the little boat toward the channel, and once in slightly deeper water I made my Le Mans start: I would head *Fiddler*'s bow a few degrees off the wind, grab the stainless steel gallows, the "rollbar" across the cockpit, make a running start, then swing myself aboard. It was only later that I realized that with all the junk in the water, and without shoes, I had taken a real chance walking the boat across the soft mud flats.

In 1613 a settlement was founded at the point where the Appomattox River meets the James. Its name was Bermuda City; it was later briefly renamed Charles City, but for centuries was known as City Point. Early in this century, it was given the name Hopewell, the name of a nearby village. For years Hopewell advertised itself as the "Chemical Capital of the South." There was a rayon plant, a nitrogen plant, and a pulp and paper mill. DuPont had a huge plant in Hopewell, as did Continental Can and Allied Chemical Corporation. After World War II, Allied Chemical contracted with another local company, the ironically named Life Science Products Company to produce kepone, a pesticide on which Allied held the patent. When in 1974 workers at the Hopewell plant exhibited serious neurological problems, scientists discovered that kepone residue had been casually discarded and had found its way through the Hopewell sewage system into the lower James. In December 1975 the James was closed to fishing. The ban lasted thirteen years, and devastated the commercial fishing and shellfishing industry on the river. Twenty years later, the Virginia Department of Health still had a fish-eating advisory in effect for the James and for its tributaries from the fall line to Hampton Roads. It was suspected that one hundred thousand pounds of kepone still rested on the bottom, and that it would remain in the bottom sediment for many decades before being neutralized by natural forces. An Environmental Protection Agency study in the late 1970s warned that dredging the contaminated sediment might pose more problems than just leaving it, and that the cost of dredging it would be staggering. Allied Chemical was fined $13.2 million, at that time the highest fine ever paid by a polluting company.

The kepone catastrophe helped galvanize people into action, and serious advances have been made in cleaning up the James. The river had been used as a sewer since the founding of Jamestown. There are sixteen major sewage treatment plants between Richmond and Norfolk; nearly 1 million gallons of treated sewage is dumped into the James daily. In the 1960s and 1970s some portions of the river, especially in its lower reaches, were not just dead, but actually toxic. But things have improved, and the day is long gone when, as happened in 1912 during an attempt to introduce a law to curb pollution in the James, one legislator went on record saying that he believed Virginia's rivers were the God-given sewers of the Commonwealth.

It didn't take long for Hopewell to be out of sight, and out of mind. The "Curles of the River" began here, a series of convoluted and complex turns and twists, all still navigable by small boats. Over the years the main channel of the river had been bypassed by a series of canals, which shortened the distance to Richmond by as much as a dozen miles. "The corkscrew," as this fourteen-mile stretch from Hopewell to Wilton also has been called, is one of the prettiest parts of the tidal James, but was given short shrift in the 1937 *Coast Pilot*. "The shores are generally wooded on both sides and present no characteristic features," the U.S. government guide read. After Hopewell, I longed for that kind of landscape.

The first "curle" began two miles above Hopewell, at Shirley Plantation. I could have scooted through Turkey Island Cutoff, one of the manmade canals, but I decided instead to lengthen the voyage by nearly five miles, and circumnavigate Turkey Island and the Presque Isle Swamp. The main house at Shirley, built in 1723, was "like a French chateau." The plantation itself, established in 1613, was one of the earliest on the James. There are no longer any wharves, and landing was out of the question. But tourists dotted the lawn, having paid the entrance fee to the attraction, which is open to the public, although ownership remains in the original family, the well-known and once fabulously rich Carters.

It was a slow but lovely sail past the shores of Turkey Island, mostly woods and swamp, and past the few houses on the mainland. When I didn't favor the outside turns, I would sometimes scratch my rudder or leeboards into the mud, but most of the time I seemed to be in fairly deep water. I had to remind myself that I was on the real James River, even though there was no traffic on these meanders except a few local fishing boats and, once in a while, a tug and barge for the sand and gravel pits at the farthest bend. A small herd of cows stood cooling off, knee-deep in the mud at the edge of one bend. The heat had become oppressive. Cumulus clouds were trying to become cumulonimbus clouds, and a thunderstorm seemed inevitable. I decided to pay more attention to my sailing, and less to the scenery.

Once back on the main river, I had only a few miles to go to what I hoped could be my anchorage for the night, an almost perfectly round sand and gravel pit, more than a quarter mile in diameter, on Curles Neck. Dodging a tug and two barges, I sailed into the anchorage just in time to set the anchor in about eight feet of water, to the sound of thunder. I lowered the mast, zipped my "back porch" tent together in record time, and waited for the first spatters. They didn't take long in arriving, but the rain was a gentle drizzle, not the violent thunderstorm for which I had prepared. Rumblings continued for hours, as did the rain, but there was little wind. Still, the air cooled off enough for me to enjoy hot soup for dinner. I had sailed about eighteen miles—with roughly fifteen miles to go to the falls. With all the twists and turns of the river in the last few days, I had yet to spend more than a few hours with the wind at my back. And after this front passed, the wind would once again shift to the northwest, where lay my destination. But the current would favor me again in the morning. The canvas tent material leaked a little, but the water that got through was not enough to keep me awake.

It was drizzling when I went to sleep, and it was drizzling when I woke up nine hours later. The cockpit seat was wet in places, as was my sleeping bag at the lower fringes. Clearing, the National Weather Service announced, wouldn't occur till later in the morning. I was in no hurry, and sailing in the rain had never appealed to me, so after breakfast I went back to bed with Middleton's *Tobacco Coast,* a maritime history of the Chesapeake.

As promised, the rain stopped by late morning, and after the fabric had dried I dismantled my tent. By now I had missed most of the flood current, and I ate lunch before heading out. Not that there was much "heading out" to be done: although the weather was cooler, the wind had not materialized, and rowing or motoring was called for. I budgeted one gallon of gas for the day, a good hour's worth. I wasn't certain about fuel further up the river, and wanted to keep a reserve in case I had trouble making my Richmond ramp appointment.

The next cutoff was Jones Neck, which saved me four miles on my trek. Here began the penultimate straight stretch of the James, near the former site of Varina—the house of Mr. and Mrs. John Rolfe, which Rolfe had named after an area in Spain admired for its fine tobacco. Rolfe and his wife, Rebecca, also known as Pocahontas, became very wealthy as a result of his tobacco cultivation and innovation. It is doubtful that Rolfe knew that his king, the very monarch after whom the river had been named, was the anonymous author of *A Counterblaste to Tobacco*, which was published in 1604, a year after James ascended the throne. "A noxious weed," the king had written, "loathsome to the eye, hateful to the nose, harmful to the brain, and dangerous to the lungs." Yet, as I had read earlier in the day, "the tobacco trade was enormously valuable to the Crown and the tobacco colonies were considered as valuable to Great Britain as the fabulously wealthy Indies to Spain."

After forty-five minutes on the glassy water, I had reached the last of the loops, Dutch Gap Cutoff, said to be the site of the first canal dug in the United States (in 1611). That first canal, quite likely dug by several of the Dutch colonists who had joined the Jamestown settlers, was extremely shallow, and probably less than a few hundred feet long. The river itself bent itself in a convoluted figure-eight shape around Farrar Island, and cutting through here saved several miles on passages. But as the river around the island silted up and became unnavigable (as it is today), a much longer canal was required to shorten the distance around Hatcher Island, now the only negotiable oxbow. The colonial ditch had probably been abandoned for nearly two centuries when the Union general Benjamin Franklin Butler made a new attempt, not so much to shorten the distance to Richmond as to allow larger warships to reach it. Confederate forces prevented this, however, and the mile-long canal was not opened until 1872, when the federal government finally finished widening and deepening the cutoff. It saved seven miles of demanding steaming or sailing.

A small sign, discreetly tucked away on the edge of the river, pointed toward the old river bend. "Richmond Yacht Basin. Fuel," it read. I checked my fuel. There was only a gallon or so left. I didn't know how current the information on the sign was, but I was happy to kill the engine and break out my oars. A mile later I found myself at a small marina with a solitary gas pump on the dock, a couple of dozen boats under a covered shed, and one small sailboat. A jovial gentleman who introduced himself as Forrest Parker filled my tiny gas tank, insisting on mixing the outboard oil to the proper proportion. He hadn't seen another sailboat in a long time, he said. When I complained that I had run out of fresh fruit, he insisted that I drive the three miles to the nearest store — in his Mercedes.

In the car, I found myself about eight miles south of Richmond, near Fort Brady, and apparently in the middle of Richmond National Battlefield Park. That explained the signs, near several private homes, that said, "No Metal Detecting. Don't Even Ask." At the country store I loaded up on fruit; then I returned Mr. Parker's car, paid for my gas, and resumed my journey.

With my mast still down, and no wind, I motored around Hatcher Island, slipping under the low, rickety pedestrian bridge on the western end of the tiny island. Once back at the upriver end of Dutch Gap Cutoff I passed by an enormous electric power plant and under an interstate highway bridge. With the current slack once more, I started rowing again. At a narrow stretch called Kingsland Reach was a small marina with a few sailboats. I hadn't used enough fuel to make a stop necessary. The river returned to its woodsy charm. Only rarely did a house interrupt its tree-lined shores. And I was only eight miles from downtown Richmond, where I would be retrieved, on the next day, from a downtown boat ramp.

There still wasn't any wind, and I continued rowing, the sun now out and beating down on me. I began thinking about an anchorage. The river had now narrowed to a width of about five hundred feet, and there were no more creeks to duck into, according to the chart. The chart did show another gravel pit, near Chaffin Bluff, but it was drawn as a lake, landlocked. Just before Chaffin Bluff, in a bend of the river, I passed a huge lawn sloping down toward the water, with an enormous but otherwise unremarkable house. In the middle of the lawn grew a massive rosette, made up of green and red plants set in concentric circles, within which ten-foot-long arrays of plants formed the letters *J* and *D*. At first I thought the initials stood for Jefferson Davis, the first and only president of the Confederate States of America. After all, Davis was buried in Richmond, and Drewry's Bluff, another high cliff a half mile upriver, had figured large in the protection of Richmond—and Davis's government—during the Civil War. (Cannon fire from the batteries on Drewry's Bluff had prevented the U.S.S. *Monitor* from reaching Richmond in 1862.) But as I was to learn later in the day, when I talked briefly with a passing fisherman, the initials stood for Jimmy Dean, the erstwhile entertainer turned "sausage king," who had built his house here staring straight down on Drewry's Bluff, the site of Fort Darling and the Confederacy's naval academy.

Just past the extravaganza, but on the opposite shore, I saw a twenty-foot-wide break in the trees along the river's edge. A lake shimmered behind the inlet, which was flanked by rocks. A cable was strung about six feet above the entrance. With my mast down I needed about four feet of vertical clearance for *Fiddler,* but even seated, I needed to duck. I shipped my oars and let the rushing current carry me into a gorgeous lagoon a thousand feet in diameter, ringed with trees. I rowed a distance along the edge until I could no longer see the opening to the river. The water was ten feet deep, and the bottom was sandy. I went for a welcome swim in the fresh, clear water, and scrubbed *Fiddler's* waterline and the deck and hatch covers. I had always liked having a boat look as good at the end of a cruise as at the beginning.

At dinner time the peace of the lagoon was shattered by a small fishing boat racing at maniacal speed through the inlet. The driver cut his throttle, and for the next hour sat patiently in one spot. Near sunset the fisherman gave up. I flagged him down. He explained the initials on the lawn on the river, and I commiserated with him on his lack of luck in the pursuit of large-mouth bass. With the sun already behind the trees he roared off, hardly slowing down at the inlet, leaving *Fiddler* rocking helplessly for several minutes on the otherwise unruffled water.

It had been a day without a sail. The mast had never even been up. The wind had never even stirred. I had gone from borrow-pit to borrow-pit. I wondered where the word *borrow-pit* came from. (It was just another word for "gravel pit.") If the sand or gravel was borrowed, it certainly had never been brought back. That suited me fine. Imagine, a hurricane-hole five miles from downtown Richmond, totally protected on all sides, with ten feet of water, and great holding ground. Of course, there was that cable at the entrance . . .

There's a description of the river written by Captain Gabriel Archer, one of the early river explorers:

> This River (we have named our kinges River) extended it self 160 myles into the mayne land betwene two fertile and fragrant bankes, two miles, a mile, & where it is least a quarter of a myle broad, navigable for shipping of 300 tunn 150 miles: the rest deep enough for small vessells of six foot draught; it ebbs and flowes 4 foote, even to the skirt of an overfall.

The "160 myles" was off by 50 miles, and the "4 foote" was wrong by almost ten inches, but it was still a remarkably accurate description, especially since a lot of the exploration had been under oar power. Having rowed a good portion of this day, I knew that there would be a tendency to overestimate. With a flexible piece of paper I measured my progress around all the bends. Five miles . . . my distance in the morning to "the skirt of an overfall" — Archer's term for the fall line.

It was so foggy at dawn that I could not have found the exit to the river without closely skirting the edge of my lagoon, barely visible a hundred feet away; but by eight o'clock the fog began to burn off and the first of the bass fishermen arrived. My time on the James was coming to an end. In the next four hours I would have to cover the remaining miles — sailing, rowing, or motoring — to meet Evelyn, and *Fiddler*'s trailer, and look for more of Smith's "faire . . . rivers."

I rowed out of my anchorage into the James. A small harbor tug and a sleek rowing shell were my only companions on the last stretch of the river. There were a few houses and several small commercial fuel docks. Near Warwick, at marker 166, the Richmond skyline came into view. Edgar Allan Poe, at age twelve, swam from Richmond to Warwick, against a rising tide, on a bet. It was one of the few bets he ever won:

Poe's gambling losses at the University of Virginia years later forced him to discontinue his studies there. Poe walked back to Richmond.

I wanted to sail to Richmond. I raised the mast, and set sail in the merest zephyr. Progress, naturally, was very slow, and by midmorning, at a red nun buoy labeled "172," the last floating navigational aid on the James, I realized that the tide had already turned against me, and I reluctantly struck sail and fired up the engine. Both shores of the river were still lined with trees. Before I turned on the engine I was able to hear the roar of the still-invisible traffic on the interstate highway that had paralleled the river since the ship terminal at Warwick. The first boulders came into view, and the first of the many Richmond bridges. Fishermen lined the banks. At the last wharf, the *Annabel Lee,* a sightseeing sternwheeler, was taking on passengers. I had last seen her at Hopewell a few days ago, although why people would want to view the waterfront at Hopewell was anybody's guess. I swung past the locks of the now-closed James River–Kanawha Canal, which for years had allowed small vessels to proceed upriver as far as Lynchburg. Another hundred yards further up the river I could see the rocky, craggy bottom begin to shoal up to meet *Fiddler*'s flat, fiberglass bottom. It was time to look for the ramp.

There were no facilities in the port of Richmond for small boats, save the ramp, which I hadn't even noticed when I had passed it earlier. The Port of Richmond is a "niche port," as it is fond of calling itself, and "the westernmost port on the North Atlantic." It handles about a half million tons of cargo a year, mostly tobacco, paper products, beer, and some scrap metal. In 1993 124 ships, some nearly five hundred feet long, made the one-hundred-mile trip from the Atlantic, most in as little as ten hours.

In the tiny, protected basin leading to the ramp, I was rewarded with something I had been hoping for during the week. I'd been hoping that somebody on the river would "speak" my vessel—a very nautical custom—and ask, "Where from?" Then I would be able to say, as mariners had for centuries, something like "Six days out of Hampton Roads."

An elderly, portly fisherman was launching a small aluminum boat from his rusty trailer. After he got it into the water, he looked at *Fiddler*, all bundled up, ready for the trailer and the highway, awaiting her turn on the inclined concrete ramp, and "spoke" us.

"Where'd you put in?"

"Hampton Roads."

"Where?" he asked in a very skeptical tone.

"Hampton Roads," I repeated. My fellow river traveler raised an eyebrow.

"How long did it take you?" Here was my chance.

"Six days. Six days out of Hampton Roads."

I had finally been able to say it. He shook his head in disbelief.

"So you stopped along the way?" He looked doubtfully at *Fiddler*.

"Every night," I said. "In little coves, quiet creeks, even a couple of gravel pits."

"You're not from around here, are you?" he asked as if that explained my bizarre travel habits. He started his outboard.

"No," I replied. "I live . . . " But I was not able to finish the sentence.

"Have a nice day," he shouted, and roared off into the James River.

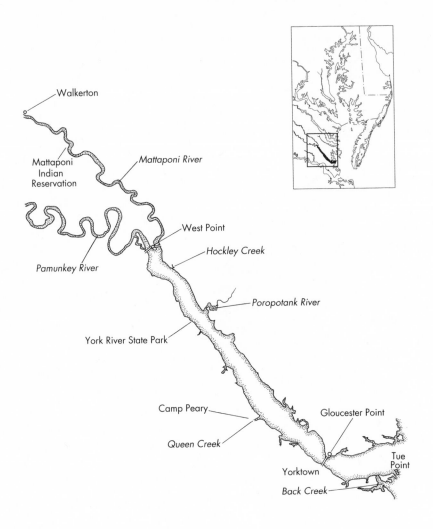

Walkerton

Mattaponi
Indian
Reservation

Mattaponi River

Pamunkey River

West Point

Hockley Creek

Poropotank River

York River State Park

Camp Peary

Queen Creek

Gloucester Point

Tue
Point

Yorktown

Back Creek

The York

*This is all I will saye to you, that suche a Baye, a Ryvar and a land
did nevar the eye of mane behould.*

—William Brewster, 1607

Back Creek, just outside the village of Dandy, had a dandy boat
ramp as close to the mouth of the York River as I could find. Back
Creek is by far the most popular name for creeks around the Chesapeake Bay: Back Creeks easily outnumber the ubiquitous Broad, Mill,
and Deep Creeks. This Back Creek, leading into a narrow passage to
the York called the Thorofare, would be the starting point for my cruise
up the York River and one of its two tributaries, the Pamunkey and the
Mattaponi. (I hadn't yet decided which.)

Captain John Smith, in his *Description of Virginia,* mentioned that
the entire river was called "Pamaunke," and was "navigable 60 or 70
myles, but with Catches and small Barkes 30 or 40 myles farther"—
a gross exaggeration that only begins to make sense if the lengths
of both branches of the river are added together. On an early map,
Robert Tindall's *Draughte of Virginia,* the York is shown as Prince Henry's
River, named after King James's eldest son. (Tindall first named today's
Gloucester Point after himself. The name Tyndall Point lasted less than
a hundred years.) The name Henry didn't stick, either, and after Henry's
death, in 1612, the name Charles River, after Prince Charles, Henry's
younger brother, was occasionally used. The appellation York came into
common use after Charles became King Charles I, and duke of York,
in 1625.

Smith had first seen the river in December 1607, and crossed both its branches after he was taken prisoner by Indians and was marched to various settlements on the Pamunkey and Mattaponi Rivers, and even on the Rappahannock, to end up on the shores of the York at the village of Werowocomoco, a dozen miles from today's town of West Point, and the home of Powhatan, "their great King," whose daughter Pocahontas saved Smith's life.

My first day on the York was a break in a record-shattering June heat wave; a cold front moving through the tidewater region the previous night had brought relief. After nearly a month of airless and oppressive weather, a welcome fresh breeze was blowing out of the northeast. My friend Bill Tatum, an airline captain and deep-water sailor, helped me launch and rig *Fiddler*.

"You know, Robert," he said. "I've never been on the York. And I've lived here on the water now for nearly a dozen years. I can't believe that." Bill, who is more at home at thirty-nine thousand feet, or in the trade winds of the Caribbean, had probably read what one of the cruising guides had to say: "We strongly recommend that yachtsmen do not spend much time above Yorktown near the mouth of the river." But I had read some other things, too. The Alliance for the Chesapeake Bay had called the York, its tributaries, and its twenty-five-hundred-square-mile drainage basin "the most pristine freshwater complex on the Atlantic coast."

"I'll let you know if you've missed anything," I said, as Bill threw me my bow line and gently pushed *Fiddler* away from the pier toward open water. I had to beat into the wind for the first half mile, but once into the Thorofare between Goodwin Neck and the low Goodwin Islands I would be on a reach. Bill was still staring out of the creek toward the York as I turned and sailed out of sight.

The two-mile-wide mouth of the York is about two dozen miles above the Virginia capes, between Tue Point and the Guinea Marshes. Tue Point, spelled Too's Point until this century, was the site of a lighthouse that stood for nearly a hundred years until it was dismantled in 1960. But the screw pile foundation was still visible two miles to the east, silhouetted against the horizon. Other structures, to the west, looked far less enticing.

To begin with, there were the enormous pier and the intimidating breakwater of the American Oil Company refinery, the only crude oil refinery in Virginia, taking deliveries of some 20 million gallons every ten days. A little further up the river an electric power plant and its chimneys dominated the landscape. A large Coast Guard facility occupied another half mile of shoreline. Two miles further on, the giant Coleman swing bridges between Yorktown and Gloucester Point kept the rest of the river hidden. The chart showed that I was sailing through a restricted anchorage marked "Explosives Handling Berth." I sailed past the evidence of the military-industrial complex as fast as I could, toward the high bluffs of Yorktown. It was nearly noon, and already the fine breeze that the front had brought was diminishing, and the temperature was increasing. A few flies found their way to *Fiddler;* and scores of jellyfish, the bay's least-loved creatures, surrounded her hull. Perhaps those cruising guides should have been heeded. But they had only cautioned about the river *beyond* Yorktown. What was I to make of all this ugliness *before* Yorktown?

A small settlement was already in existence here in the 1650s. Yorktown was officially established in 1691; and by 1750 it had a population of between two thousand and three thousand. It became an important tobacco port and experienced steady growth until the Revolution. William Eddis wrote from Yorktown in 1769:

> I will begin with acquainting you that the situation of this town is exquisitely beautiful, and the adjacent country very romantic and picturesque. The noble Chesapeake is full in view, which, in the narrowest part, is at least ten miles broad, and runs of near three hundred [sic], navigable for the largest ships. Many considerable rivers discharge themselves into this bay, by which advantages of commerce are extended to the interior country; and planters whose habitations are far remote from the ocean receive at their own doors by water conveyance the various productions of distant nations.

Twelve years later, Yorktown was receiving some very unwelcome "productions of distant nations." The town was already in an economic decline, and the siege to which it was subjected in 1781 completed its downfall, even as it ensured it a permanent and prominent place in history.

The siege of Yorktown began on September 28 and ended three weeks later with the surrender by Lieutenant General Lord Charles Cornwallis on October 19, after the last major battle of the American Revolution. During those three weeks more than fifty British ships ended up on the bottom of the York, some sunk by cannon fire, and others set on fire and sailed toward the French fleet, but most intentionally scuttled to keep them out of enemy hands. In the 1980s the Virginia Department of Conservation and Historic Resources, led by John Broadwater, the Commonwealth's first underwater archaeologist, began surveying, then excavating, a number of the British navy ships.

Broadwater called the York River "an archaeologist's nightmare, beset by strong and unpredictable tidal currents, near-zero visibility, and persistent stinging jellyfish." I hoped it wasn't turning into a sailor's nightmare. I'd seen the jellyfish, and now I began to experience the current, not very strong, but against me. And of course the current was worse where the river was narrow and deep: my exact location.

The bridge at Yorktown, the only bridge across the river, was opened in 1952. The river is narrowest here, only 2,000 feet wide, but it is very deep — 70 and 80 feet, and more in places. The U.S. Navy, with the Yorktown Naval Mine Depot and other large ship facilities and anchorages, required enormous vertical clearance for its vessels, making a swing bridge the only practical solution. But the navy ships also required an unprecedented horizontal clearance: 450 feet. With the depths approaching 90 feet, two bridges would be required, each pivoting on its own support, and each providing half of the required clearance.

Although Yorktown was no longer a tobacco port, its economic decline had been halted, and reversed, owing to the creation in 1936 of the National Colonial Historical Park, one of the most popular tourist attractions in tidewater Virginia; as well as to an increasing military presence during and after World War II, and most recently, the growth of the suburbs, and the exodus to the country.

The swing bridges, closed, could handle several *Fiddler*s stacked on top of one another. I slowly squeaked by the Yorktown waterfront and its narrow, steep-to beach, too exposed and vulnerable for beaching a Dovekie. Waves from passing boats could throw *Fiddler* up on the beach, and I didn't stop. Lunch would have to wait.

Before the bridge was built, a ferry operated between Yorktown and Gloucester Point. The ferry service, started in 1705, remained in continuous operation (except during the Yorktown siege) for two and a half centuries. In 1705 a half dozen ferries were serving on the York and its tributaries. By 1720 several more had been added. Crossing from Yorktown to Gloucester Point cost sixpence for a man, and one shilling for a man and a horse. In 1940, with Yorktown's population hovering around three hundred, the ferry ran every half hour, and the cost for a car and driver was fifty cents, with an additional fifteen cents for each passenger.

I left several sailboats behind, not because I outpaced them, but because they decided to stay on the windward side of the bridge. Lunch became snacks and fruit, as I doggedly tried to gain some distance up-river. I wasn't suffering, but I wasn't having the sail of a lifetime, either. On the north side of the river were several low marshes: the Mumfort, Carmines, and Catlett Islands. Yet I stuck to the southern shore, because I had started thinking about Queen Creek, just past King Creek, and just past the navy's restricted anchorage, as a possible spot to spend the night.

Except for the Naval Weapons Station and the Naval Supply Center, the southern shore of the York was undisturbed, and mostly wooded. The summer sun was glaring, and I was glad that *Fiddler* had a tanbark sail, which was much easier on the eyes than a white one. Keeping an eye on the sail was the one constant in my life. Around two, I was glad to see, the breeze picked up again. The entrance to Queen Creek was a little more than five miles from Yorktown, and by midafternoon I was past the navy installations and nearing the entrance to the creek. West Point, the town at the head of the river, sat a good twenty miles further to the northwest—only the broad, watery horizon was visible in that direction.

For two centuries and more, until it silted up, Queen Creek was used by small vessels as a back door to Williamsburg. The three-mile trip could take hours, as a diary entry by John Fontaine (an Irish visitor to Virginia in the eighteenth century) made clear on another June day:

> June 5, 1715. Sunday. We set sail in the morning [from Gloucester] and we had a fresh gale, as much as we could carry sail. About 12 we came to Queen's Creek and about 3 we came to the landing of Williamsburg and I left the men in the boat and went up to the town which is about a mile from the landing place.

I had not planned to go to Williamsburg, although in a boat like *Fiddler* I could still probably get to within a mile of it, but the creek looked well protected, and would be a private anchorage. It also turned out to be pretty. Since Yorktown I had not seen another boat, and on Queen Creek (the *s* was dropped some years ago) that solitude continued. With marsh on one side, and woods on the other, the winding creek presented stunning vistas at each turn. Only two things reminded me that much had changed since Fontaine's visit: a parade of navigational markers, and—on the marshy side of the creek—a series of small signs every hundred yards or so, cryptically marked "No Trespassing. Government Property." Officially called Camp Peary Military Reservation, the area is reportedly used by the Central Intelligence Agency as a training facility, as Tom Clancy readers learned from Clancy's first techno-thriller. The agency would, as is its custom, neither confirm nor deny it.

I went as far as marker 15, and then saw up ahead on a bend in the creek a small marina with several sheds and piers, and a few small sailboats. Since I didn't need anything except privacy, I struck the sail and motored back toward the entrance, where I hoped that during the night there would be more of a breeze, which would help to keep insects away. I noted that seven of the fifteen daymarkers I passed had osprey nests on them. The birds favored red markers over green ones by a ratio of four to three. I pondered the significance of that, having just read the night before that 22 percent of the ospreys in the Chesapeake area nest on aids to navigation. I decided that it only proved that the Chesapeake Bay was the world's most studied estuary.

I anchored off the channel in four feet of water, took a quick swim, and started thinking about supper. The air cooled off nicely, and a little breeze made me chance sleeping without being tented in. After sunset, the wake of a late-returning fishing skiff helped rock me to sleep.

The wake of an early-departing boat helped awaken me at sunrise. The night had been free of insects, and my inflatable mattress and sleeping bag had given me a comfortable night. There was dew, but not enough to have soaked me. It was a little before six on this Saturday morning, and clearly the Williamsburg suburbanites were hitting the fishing grounds with a vengeance, for within the hour a half dozen more boats had sped by my anchorage.

I checked the pan I had dangled overboard on a line after my dinner the previous night. This was a trick a waterman had once told me about. "The crabs will have cleaned it by morning," he had said. They had. By seven o'clock *Fiddler* had a cool, brisk breeze from the north, and we were on our way.

Not for long, however. I had barely managed to make one tack across the river toward Blundering Point when the breeze failed. But it didn't quite fail enough to spare me a whiff of West Point, which I smelled at about the same time as I saw its chimneys—fifteen miles ahead. These belonged to the paper and pulp plant of the Chesapeake Corporation, and for the next day or so they would dominate the horizon.

The York here was a little more than two miles wide, and wouldn't vary much in width until it reached its end at West Point. Any movement I was making toward that goal, however, was mostly caused by the current. Around midmorning I saw in the distance a small, triangular red sail headed downriver toward me. It hardly had any wind either, so it took some time for us to come close enough for identification. Another Dovekie? It couldn't be. Or could it? At a half mile distance I thought I could make out leeboards on the sides of the hull. When we finally glided past each other I saw that it was a little boat called a Cartopper, another Philip Bolger design, with a raked mast, a spritsail, and leeboards just like *Fiddler*'s. Its skipper and I waved to each other.

There wasn't much to do, and it was too hot to row. The scenery was pleasant, though: beautiful, tree-lined shores, few houses, and a blessed absence of military architecture. By noon I had been carried as far as York River State Park, at Croaker Point. It was a "slick calm," as the watermen would have said. I really needed only two things: shade and a trash can. The park would provide both. I ran *Fiddler* up on the little beach next to the boat ramp, which was seeing hectic activity by weekend fishermen, and then anchored her a little distance off the shore in a foot of water and waded ashore with my lunch. For the next three hours I sat underneath a big shade tree, tried to catch what zephyrs I could, and waited for more favorable current, or more wind, and any cooling of the stifling heat.

John Fontaine had a very different experience on the York River, as his diary reveals:

> April 22, 1718. I went down to Williamsburg to Mr. Maury, and hired a Flat [flat-bottomed boat], after I had bought the Rum and Molasses he wanted.

> April 25, 1718. The goods were embarked and we went out of Queen's Creek, and went to the Oyster Banks, where we took in a great many oysters, and came about 6 miles up the river. We came

as close [to] the land as we could and stuck an oar in the mud, and tied our flat to it, where we lay till 'twas day. A cold place.

April 26, 1718. Took up our oar and rowed about four miles. The wind at N W, blew very hard. We were blown in on the flats, and sea was so high, and no possibility of landing, so that we were obliged to throw what oysters we had overboard to lighten the boat. Shipped a great deal of water, and having no anchor we were like to drive on the mud and loose the flat. About two of the clock the weather calming, we set out again and made about five miles, but the wind came to N W such a violent storm that we were obliged to put before the wind, and when we had gone back a mile, we ran the flat ashore upon the strand, where we thumped mightily. The wind continued very hard, but the tide being fallen, we unloaded the goods, expecting that when the boat would float, she would beat to pieces, so that about twelve at night, we had all our goods on shore, but there being no house near, we lay upon the strand all night. It rained hard and wet us to the skin, but the wind abated, and when the tide came in, we halled our flat up as far as we could and received no damage but being wet both with fresh and salt water.

April 27, 1718. About 6 in the morning, being Sunday, we put the goods on board and half an hour after the wind blew hard at northwest, so that about 12 it abated and we set out and reached West Point about nine of the clock.

By midafternoon I'd made my way back to the boat. A small breeze had sprung up. The tide was now dead low. What I had forgotten was that the current change lagged two or three hours behind the times of low and high tide, or at least did so here. And so, an hour and a half later I found myself still only a mile from the state park. But I had on this early summer's day more than four hours of daylight left to find a cool anchorage.

Eventually, as it always does, the current slacked and I was able to make some progress, though at a snail's pace. A sailboat twice *Fiddler's*

size was motorsailing toward West Point, and then dropped all pretense
and sails. Soon we were alone again on the river, I hot and sticky, *Fiddler*
hardly moving.

And then I saw a mirage. Up ahead, near Belleview, a small settlement on the north shore of the York, I spotted what looked like a beer
truck. Huge red letters spelling "Coors" soon stood out on the side
turned toward the water. It was no mirage. It was a real beer truck,
and it stood on the edge of a real beach. A half dozen motorboats were
moored on the edge of the beach. There was a large tent, and clusters
of people were milling about. Here was a chance, I thought, to buy a
cold beer.

I ran *Fiddler,* under sail, onto the gently sloping beach and hopped
out.

"Is there a store here? Can I buy a cold beer?" I asked some people
standing around in bathing suits with cold beers in their hands.

"No store here," a man with a beer belly and a ponytail answered.
"This is a private beach party."

Having had my first question answered, I asked the second question again.

"No," came the reply. "Unless you buy one of these." He pointed to
a fluorescent-green plastic wristband. "Fifteen bucks."

"For one beer?"

"You can drink all you want till ten tonight." Several bystand-
ers appeared to commiserate with me, but no offers were forthcoming.
Who knew? I might have been a Virginia Alcoholic Beverage Control
inspector disguised as a beach-cruising sailor.

I turned the boat around in the shallow water and ostentatiously
did my Le Mans start, which was by now well practiced. There was just
enough wind to make it look impressive. I had hoped to hear applause,
and maybe shouts signaling a change of mind, but it was not to be. I
drank a warm seltzer and continued on my way. By five the York had
completely run out of wind, and I had run out of patience.

I anchored in five feet of water between the York River Channel light and a beautiful marsh at the mouth of Bakers and Hockley Creeks. I swam and bathed, then scrubbed the hull's waterline. Although the water was nearly fresh, I saw two large jellyfish, but they were easily spotted and avoided. All the little jellyfish had disappeared.

After dinner a welcome breeze sprang up, but because the current was now opposing the breeze, my open roadstead anchorage became very boisterous, and I moved into the mouth of Hockley Creek, never sounding less than six feet. I didn't tent myself in, as it was still too hot for that. And if it did get buggy so close to the marsh, getting back into the wide York would be easy, even after dark.

A brisk breeze and cool temperatures greeted me in the morning. After a leisurely Sunday breakfast I sailed the short distance to West Point and the end of the York.

At West Point, the York River meets its headwaters. "At the ordinary flowing of the salt water, it divideth it selfe into two gallant branches," John Smith had written in his *Description of Virginia*. These were the Pamunkey and the Mattaponi Rivers, both navigable for extraordinary distances. A hundred years ago, the Pamunkey could still be navigated for about fifty miles, and the Mattaponi for an astonishing eighty-eight miles above West Point. Today the practical head of navigation for both rivers is about twenty-five miles. Geographers consider the Mattaponi to be the real headwaters of the York, perhaps because it is longer. Perhaps that's one reason I decided to go up the Mattaponi.

The Pamunkey is formed by the North and South Anna Rivers, and the Little River. The Mattaponi is fed by three branches shown on some maps as the Matta, the Po, and the Ni—a disingenuous display on the part of the cartographer, since the name Mattaponi is mentioned in the earliest communications from Virginia. Three-fourths of the watershed is forested (the Chesapeake Corporation is the largest single owner), while most of the remainder is in pasture, or planted in crops.

West Point had the sorriest-looking waterfront I'd seen since Hopewell. Its press hadn't been too favorable, either. *A Cruising Guide to the*

Chesapeake had pulled no punches: "Unlike its famous namesake on the Hudson, the West Point on the York River, 35 miles above the entrance, is low, commercial, and unattractive. A paper and pulp plant is said to 'emit a foul odor' at times, which even floats down the river a way on northwesterly winds." I remembered.

I tied up at a ramshackle pier tenuously attached to a waterfront bar-and-restaurant that looked positively hung over. But away from the waterfront, the town turned out to be charming, with tree-lined streets and an eclectic collection of buildings. It was still nearly deserted this early in the morning. The plastic-wrapped Sunday newspapers were lying untouched on the lawns, and an unusual number of cats prowled the streets and gardens. The few pedestrians whom I met smiled and nodded. It was a pleasant place for a constitutional.

The only place that was open was the fire and rescue station. I chatted with one of the volunteers about the rivers and made the mistake of commenting on the overwhelming physical presence—and smell—of the paper plant. My informant looked very annoyed: "If it wasn't for them, we wouldn't be here," he said. I got the message: this was definitely a company town. The Works Projects Administration guide to Virginia, published in 1940, alluded to this when it noted, "The olfactory nerves of local residents seem immune to the odor that other York River people, who have suffered because polluted water has brought about decline of the once profitable oyster business, find objectionable."

The "West" in West Point had nothing to do with the compass point. The town was named for the four West brothers, Thomas, Francis, Nathaniel, and John—three of whom were governors of Virginia—but especially for John West, who patented the land between the Pamunkey and the Mattaponi. In 1691 West Point was made a port of entry, and soon thereafter it was renamed Delaware, in honor of John West, who had become the third Lord Delaware. It was seriously considered as a possible capital of Virginia when the growth of the colony's population made the current capital, Williamsburg, inconvenient. When, in 1861, the railroad was completed between the town and Richmond, the town was renamed West Point.

The Lord Delaware swing bridge over the Mattaponi would not swing open except on twenty-four hour's notice. When it was closed, its vertical clearance was twelve feet, but it was a simple matter to lower *Fiddler*'s mast and row into the Mattaponi River. I made the choice between going up the Mattaponi or going up the Pamunkey somewhat arbitrarily. The Mattaponi was longer, but had somewhat less current and seemed more rural. And if I went up the Pamunkey, I would have to go past the paper plant, which I had now experienced for long enough. The smoke from its chimneys was blowing horizontally, a reliable indicator that winds, at least those at high elevations, were blowing fifteen or more miles per hour.

The Mattaponi, naturally deep for a very long distance, had already begun to silt up by the middle of the eighteenth century, and by 1788 the Virginia Assembly had ordered it "cleared and improved" to give it "a sufficient depth and width of water to navigate boats, batteaus, or canoes, capable of carrying four hogsheads of tobacco." This dredging was periodically done in the upper reaches of the river until the 1930s, by which time river traffic had declined so severely that the occasional maintenance dredging was suspended.

But for the first dozen miles or so, water depths would not be a problem, even for very large boats. The chart showed depths, especially on the sharper bends, of thirty and forty feet. I raised the mast, unfurled the sail, and with a favoring current started my cruise up one of the "gallant branches" of the York.

There was not a stretch of the Mattaponi anywhere along its length which was straight for more than a half mile. And for nearly its entire serpentine length the river—an ever-changing, ever-curving, pristine ribbon of nearly fresh water which nevertheless remained tidal for more than thirty miles—was lined by marshes, by woods, or by meadows. Although narrow, seldom more than a thousand feet wide, the river offered wide and unexpected vistas as *Fiddler* negotiated its twists and turns on a lively breeze.

I had met only one small motorboat all morning. Once past Water-fence Landing (with a depth of forty-six feet) and a gorgeous estate called Chelsea Farm, I passed the mouth of a small tributary stream called Heartquake Creek (with a depth of 53 feet!). The chart noted that fishermen would henceforth be required to have a Virginia fishing license. We were in fresh water. This was the official transition from the merely brackish to the totally fresh.

The English settlers noted that the American Indians often used place names to identify their tribes—and vice versa. As mentioned earlier, the York River was initially called the Paumaunke, after a tribe. The Mattaponi Indians who lived along this river were a small tribe of the Powhatan Confederacy, as were many other tribes whose names are still reflected in our geography: Pawtuxunt, Toppahanock, Patawomeke, Appamatuck, Nandsamund, Chesapeack. John Smith mentioned "on the North branch [the] Mattapament, who have 30 men"—a tribe of perhaps a hundred souls, including the warriors. By 1781 the tribe had only fifteen or twenty members, living on a tiny reservation ten miles up the river.

After a pleasant and occasionally exciting morning sail, I ran *Fiddler* up on a sand-and-gravel beach on one of the very sharp bends in the river. It was nearly noon, and I searched among my provisions for the makings of an appropriate Sunday lunch. Just as I was completing a tuna-fish-and-cucumber experiment I heard the roar of a motorboat. From around the bend a boat sped toward my peaceful picnic grounds. Afraid that its wake would grind a lot of gravel into *Fiddler*'s hull, I quickly floated the boat into deeper water away from the shore. But wonder of wonders, the motorboat cut its throttle, allowed its wake to dissipate, and then approached slowly and in a seamanlike manner.

"How long have you had your Dovekie?" *Fiddler*'s unique lineage had again been recognized, and a long conversation ensued about shoal-draft boats in general, and sharpies in particular. My interrogator told me that he often spent his weekends putt-putting, with his wife, on the

waters within reach of his native Richmond, but hoped to "really explore" them once he acquired a small cruising sailboat. A Dovekie was
one of the candidates, but by the time they left I think it had become the
only candidate. I dragged *Fiddler* back onto the beach again and resumed
my lunch.

When more boat traffic appeared I resumed my sail. First there
were some jet skis—"personal watercraft," as they are called—scooting
mindlessly up and down the river; then there were a few powerful speedboats that moved just as mindlessly, only faster. As I made my way up the
river on a fickle, faltering breeze, with *Fiddler* bouncing off the various
wakes, the reason for all this activity became clear: I was approaching
a camping resort called Rainbow Acres. "Nettle-free swimming," I later
read in its brochure, was one of its attractions.

I anchored *Fiddler* in knee-deep water and walked ashore. Rainbow
Acres played host to numerous watersports enthusiasts on weekends,
but its mainstay was providing space, and some facilities, for about 150
trailers, all lined up along a few sandy lanes named—what else?—Rappahannock, Potomac, York, and James Avenues. I bought some groceries
in the general store and then walked back to the boat. The current was
still not favorable, but enough wind had sprung up to make the rest of
the afternoon's sail demanding, even memorable.

Around another sharp bend in the river I reached the half mile of
riverfront belonging to the Mattaponi Indian Reservation, which consisted of fewer than two hundred acres—all that remained of the Matta-
ponis' once-huge territory. Along with the nine-hundred-acre reservation on the Pamunkey River, it was all that was left to the Indians after
the English settlers occupied the tidewater region. Thomas Jefferson in
1787 mentioned that the Mattaponi tribe had only "3-4 men" and the
Pamunkeys numbered only "10-12 men."

I struck sail, maneuvered *Fiddler* toward the dilapidated wharf, and
managed to tie her so that she was protected from the wakes of the
hyperactive stinkpotters. Then I walked up the steep slope that apparently also did duty as an oversized boat ramp. A few teenagers sat on the

back of a pickup truck and waved to me when I walked by. I waved back.

The village was tiny and did not look prosperous. Two or three dozen dwellings, mostly mobile homes, were interspersed with vegetable gardens, junked cars, a small white Baptist church, a general store that was closed on Sunday, and the Mattaponi Museum, which Norman Custalow was about to close for the day. Custalow's real name is Evening Star, and he is the chief of the Mattaponi tribe, in which about 300 Indians claim membership, although only about 125 live on the reservation.

Chief Evening Star was in his sixties, dressed in leisure pants and sport shirt. Affable and accommodating, he agreed to keep the museum open a little longer, and after paying the seventy-five-cent admission fee I was given a short tour of the tiny building, which was packed to the rafters with Indian paraphernalia, memorabilia, prints and photographs, and a necklace said to have belonged to Pocahontas. The Indians do not pay state taxes, the chief told me, and they are exempt from hunting and fishing license fees. Each year around Thanksgiving a delegation from the tribe travels to Richmond and presents the governor with a deer, a turkey, or a mess of fish as a tribute, a custom that dates from a treaty made in 1646. Until recently, many of the tribesmen were shad fishermen and hunting guides, but both occupations have seen better days.

It was getting late in the day. I thanked Chief Evening Star and mentioned that I would like to come back some time, by car, and spend more time in the museum.

"Where *is* your car?" the Chief asked. I told him I'd come by boat, a sailboat, and I still had to find an anchorage for the night. "I've had people here from all over, even England and Russia," he said. "But nobody's ever come here by boat!" I completed my circumambulation of the village and headed back to the wharf.

The further I traveled away from Rainbow Acres and its boat ramp, and the later it got, the quieter the river became, and during the evening I was only once disturbed by a homeward-rushing speedboat.

The lively breeze lasted until late evening. Sometimes reaching what appeared to be six knots, *Fiddler* swooped around all the bends, the marshy shore alternating with stands of trees on both sides of the river. A housing development of minor proportions seemed to be in the making near Mantapike, in King and Queen County, on the north side of the river; and occasionally a single dwelling appeared among the trees on the high banks. Navigation became a bit confusing along a few miles of the river called De Farges Bar, where the river's course offered several possibilities. Not having to worry about draft, I just sailed the boat on a meandering course between the many little islands that dotted the river.

Near sundown I anchored between two of the islands, in complete solitude. Because the current was especially strong, I rigged a long line behind the boat with a flotation cushion, and held on to the safety line when I went for a swim. The water seemed particularly clear and clean. The water temperature was refreshingly cool, and as the sun dipped behind the trees beyond miles of marshes, I was glad I had brought some fall clothing, on this summer's day. At sunset a small fishing boat came roaring by in the main channel. It was the last boat I saw on the river.

My last day on this tributary of the York River turned out to be hazy and windless. It had been very cool the night before, but there had been no dew, and the day promised to be a scorcher. I had made arrangements to be hauled out later in the day at Walkerton, about twenty-five miles above West Point and sixty miles above the entrance of the York. I planned, if the day were to remain windless, to begin motoring to my destination, about six miles upriver. If I ran out of fuel before getting there, I would row the rest of the way; with luck, the current would be with me. Actually, I thought about rowing the last mile or so regardless of the status of my gas tank, if only to impress my compatriot and friend Wil van Werkhoven, who, I hoped, would be waiting at the ramp.

I swam again, with my safety line firmly attached to the boat. After breakfast I broke out the anchor and then rowed for a mile. The river's favorable current increased my rowing speed to three miles per hour, but after twenty minutes I started the engine for the final leg of the trip.

The stream now became very narrow but was bordered by wide

marshes, beyond which were high banks. There were few houses here, and those few were carefully hidden among the trees on the fifty- or sixty-foot-high banks. They all had long steps leading down to small piers, and runabouts.

Walkerton, busy with logging and sawmills until fifty years ago, has the distinction of having the greatest tidal range of any place on the Chesapeake—3.9 feet, as much as the tidal range on the Atlantic Ocean at the Virginia capes, more than eighty miles to the southeast.

If I had chosen to continue my cruise I could have gone under the swing bridge at Walkerton (since *Fiddler* can make do with a five-foot vertical clearance) toward Aylett, another village eight miles up the river, and probably some distance beyond, especially on the tide, as had been possible when Europeans first settled here.

A mile or so from Walkerton I shut the engine down and began rowing again. There still wasn't a breath of air. As I approached the bridge I spotted the ramp, but neither Wil nor *Fiddler*'s trailer. Alas, my rowing prowess was not to be admired. I allowed *Fiddler* to drift into the pier next to the ramp on the east side of the bridge. After I had gotten the boat ready for her trip on the highway, I walked over to the store that stood next to the bridge, and across the road from the ramp.

"A tourist," the famous solo sailor Ann Davison had once written, "remains an outsider throughout his visit, but a sailor is part of the local scene from the moment he arrives." There wasn't much left of the local scene—just the store owner and the Dr Pepper salesman.

"Been at least a year or two since the bridge's been opened," said the owner of the Baldwin Supermarket in answer to my query. "They want to know a bunch of days ahead, and don't like to do it even then."

In the next year, he said, a new fixed bridge would be built with a twenty-two-foot clearance. This meant that the road would be more than twenty feet above his store, and access to the store would be very difficult, and certainly inconvenient. Would it hurt his business? I asked.

"Sure," he said. "Well, probably. But I'm ready to get retired. I'm already tired." He rang up the amount—a quarter—for the cup of coffee I had poured myself.

Before I could finish the cup, Wil and *Fiddler*'s trailer arrived. As *Fiddler* was ratcheted on the trailer, a fresh breeze sprang up from the southwest. Just before the bow slid up on the first roller, *Fiddler* yawed, and I had to slide her off the trailer a short distance to straighten her out. "She wants to go back in," Wil said. "So do I," I said.

Hilaire Belloc had written, à propos of rivers, "They lead us along nowither, and yet are alive with discovery, emotion, adventure, peril, and response."

Someday I would discover whether the Pamunkey was as pretty as the Mattaponi.

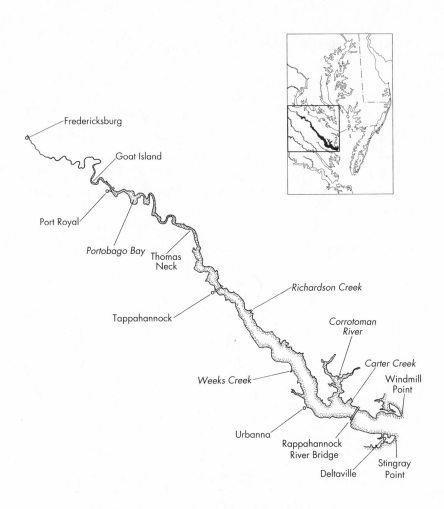

Fredericksburg

Goat Island

Port Royal

Portobago Bay

Thomas Neck

Richardson Creek

Tappahannock

Corrotoman River

Carter Creek

Windmill Point

Weeks Creek

Urbanna

Rappahannock River Bridge

Deltaville

Stingray Point

The Rappahannock

A river is more than an amenity, it is a treasure. It offers a necessity of life that must be rationed among those who have the power over it.

—Oliver Wendell Holmes, 1931

The Rappahannock River rises from its headwaters on the eastern slopes of the Blue Ridge Mountains and travels, ever widening, for two hundred miles, toward the Chesapeake Bay. Its mouth, four miles wide, lies between two spits of land, Windmill Point and Stingray Point. Windmill Point didn't receive its name until well into the eighteenth century, when many rivers on the Chesapeake Bay had the distinctive structures, but Stingray Point was named in July 1608, although it was at first misnamed Stingray Isle.

On June 2, 1608, Captain John Smith had set out, along with fourteen other men, on his first voyage to explore the Chesapeake Bay. His boat was a "strong ribb'd bark" of two or three tons' burden (there are conflicting accounts)—an open barge probably around thirty feet long, which could be rowed and sailed. That voyage (there was to be a second one later in the year) lasted seven weeks, and took Smith from the mouth of the Chesapeake north along the Eastern Shore; then, skirting the western shore above the Patuxent River, he went to within twenty miles of the head of the bay, before turning south again. He spent a month exploring the Potomac and then turned homeward toward Jamestown. On the extensive flats on the southern shore of the entrance to the Rappahannock, the barge was caught by the ebb tide, and grounded out. While waiting for the flood tide to float them off again, Smith and his crew amused themselves by spearing fish, but Smith was himself speared by a stingray as he was taking the creature off his blade. As related by two members of the crew:

> Having finished this discovery, (though our victuall was neere spent) he intended to see his imprisonment-acquaintances upon the river of Rapahanock, by many called Toppahanock, but our bote by reason of the ebbe, chansing to grownd upon a many shoules lying in the entrances, we spyed many fishes lurking in the reedes: our Captaine sporting himselfe by nayling them to the grownd with his sword, set us all a fishing in that manner: thus we tooke more in one houre then we could eate in a day. But it chansed our Captaine taking a fish from his sword (not knowing her condition) being much of the fashion of a Thorneback, but with a long tayle, like a ryding rodde, whereon the middest is a most poysoned sting, of two or three inches long, beared like a saw on each side, which she strucke into the wrest of his arme neere an inch and a halfe: no bloud nor wound was seene, but a little blew spot, but the torment was instantly so extreame, that in foure hours had so swolen his hand, arme and shoulder, we all with much sorrow concluded his funerall, and prepared his grave in an Island hard by, as himselfe directed: yet it pleased God by a precious oyle Docter Russell at the first applyed to it when he sounded it with probe (ere night) his tormenting paine was so well asswaged that he eate of the fish to his supper, which gave no lesse joy and content to us then ease to himselfe, for which we called the Island Stingray Isle after the name of the fish.

Thus the account of the incident written by Walter Russell and Anas Todkill in the *Proceedings of the English Colony.* Smith had suffered a severe toxic reaction. The expedition returned to Jamestown immediately. The Rappahannock's exploration would have to wait until the second voyage of discovery.

Just north of the mouth of the Rappahannock is a small creek called Antipoison Creek. Folklore has it that the Indians living on the creek provided the antidote to the "poison" that nearly killed Smith. The tale has been told over and over again in countless books and articles, but the real story is far more interesting than the folk etymology would suggest. It is most likely that *Antipoison* is a corruption of an Indian word that has nothing to do with "poison."

The stingray is not fished commercially, as researchers at the Virginia Institute of Marine Science have urged for years: one marine biologist has remarked that it is delicious: "reminiscent of pork, but more delicate."

After a few days in Jamestown, Smith set out again, this time with twelve crew members, in the last week of July. They went straight north to the head of the bay as far as the Susquehanna River, and then, after exploring the Sassafras "and all the inlets and rivers worth noting," turned south, exploring the Patuxent, and finally the Rappahannock.

"It is an excellent, pleasant, well inhabited, fertill, and a goodly navigable river," two of the crew members later wrote. The Rappahannock is navigable for ninety-three miles from the mouth (Smith says "some 130 myles"), as far as present-day Fredericksburg.

It was not an easy journey. They buried one crew member on the shore of a place they called Fetherstones Bay, after the deceased. It is impossible to reconstruct from the description where that might have been. Miraculously, the rest of the expedition's members remained healthy: "Notwithstanding their ill dyet, and bad lodging, crowded in so small a Barge, in so many dangers never resting, but always tossed to and againe . . . wee sayled so high as our Boat would float, there setting up crosses, and graving our names in the trees."

I wasn't planning to set up any crosses or scribble graffiti along the way. And I knew how high up the river my boat would float: "Strangers," the *Coast Pilot* stated with authority, "can safely carry a draft of 8 feet to Fredericksburg with the aid of a chart." I had a chart, and my sharpie *Fiddler* had a draft of only four inches with the leeboards and rudder up. On a hot and humid August morning I set out to find a launching ramp for *Fiddler* as close as possible to Stingray Point.

I found a rough gravel ramp at the J&M Marina on Broad Creek, near Deltaville, less than a mile from Stingray Point. Deltaville likes to call itself the "Boatbuilding Capital of the Chesapeake," and there was indeed a lot of boating and boatbuilding activity all around the town. The charge for launching was five dollars.

"When will you be back?" said the lady near the ramp who, I suspected, was either the *J* or the *M* of the enterprise.

"I'm not coming back," I said. "I'm headed for Fredericksburg." I was waiting to hear something about rapids around, say, Port Royal, but all I got was a smile. It occurred to me that since I wasn't returning to the ramp I should only have to pay half of the five-dollar fee. I tried to haggle, but it didn't work. She thought my argument very funny.

"It's five whether you come back or not. Have a nice trip."

"Nice try," my friend Shelby Creagh said. He helped me to launch *Fiddler* into her element and drove off with the trailer.

I had a goal of moving twelve or fifteen miles a day. That would give me a week or so on the river. But on this first day, with a late start, I hoped to cover about half that distance before looking for an anchorage.

I motored out of Broad Creek into the broad Rappahannock River. The lighthouse at Stingray Point was barely visible on the horizon—rather, the remains of the lighthouse were visible, for the superstructure had been removed decades earlier, leaving only a screw pile foundation on which the Coast Guard had placed a small beacon, leaving the structure looking rather naked.

It was warm, but a building breeze appeared out of the northeast. Once out of the creek into the river, I made sail and very slowly moved toward the first of the three bridges that spanned the Rappahannock's navigable portion: at Whitestone, a half dozen miles upriver; at Tappahannock, some twenty miles upstream; and at Port Royal, sixty-some miles away. The day was hazy, and the water appeared hazy, for the river brimmed with jellyfish, more than I'd ever seen before, looking—as John Barth wrote in *The Tidewater Tales*—"like a billion old condoms with their miserable sting and beautiful name *Chrysaora quinquecirrha.*"

The *Maryland Gazette* in 1750 reported that a man had fallen overboard in the Rappahannock River and had been drowned after being entangled "in a great number of Sea nettles." Stingrays were the least of the Rappahannock's problems.

In 1688 the Reverend John Clayton described jellyfish as "like a Jelly, or Starch that is made with a cast of Blue in it . . . downwards there are long fibrous strings, some whereof I have found near half a Yard long." But as Arthur Pierce Middleton pointed out, "these creatures caused a great deal of suffering in the Chesapeake, generally of too minor a nature to find its way into the annals of history: fishermen, oystermen, mariners, and bathers frequently felt the sting of the picric acid in the streamers of jellyfish."

I looked forward to reaching the fresher waters of the river on my journey toward its fall line, for in fresh water the critters would be absent. But Chesapeake Bay swimmers should count their blessings: some species of medusa grow tentacles to a length of 120 feet. It is scant relief to learn that most jellyfish live only about one to three months. Chesapeake Bay swimmers may not know that there is an edible species — *Rhopilema esculenta,* of eastern Asian waters, which is prized by the Japanese and Chinese — and probably hope that harvest of the local species would reduce the pests. Jellyfish are thought to perform a scavenging function, but sometimes it is difficult to feel forgiving, especially given their occasionally rampant concentration. Still, they are beautiful. Ruskin reminded us "that the most beautiful things in the world are the most useless; peacocks and lilies for instance."

The breeze nudged me along the southern shore of the river, toward the northwest. Summer cottages littered the shore, and for all I knew, they were now winterized for year-round use. Some new houses were under construction, but they seemed oblivious to notions of scale, and landscape, and unembarrassed by their intrusion on the otherwise beautiful waterfront.

I saved several miles by cutting across the flats surrounding the dredged mouth of Broad Creek. With the wind behind me I skirted the shore closely, and scared an osprey from its nest atop a sign that said, in print too small for me to read until I was too close: "Danger. Submerged

Rocks." I missed the rocks, and was sorry to have disturbed the fishhawk. The wind remained light, but after the middle of the afternoon the current helped to give us a bit of a push. The bluffs on shore became a bit higher and the cottages even more closely spaced. To my relief, however, after about three miles some open spaces appeared, some honest-to-God farms, and some "unimproved" land. There were no developments on the opposite shore, two or three miles away. On my port side there were several little creeks suitable for *Fiddler*'s draft: Sturgeon, Hunting, and Woods Creeks. I decided to sail between Parrott Island and the mainland, where the chart showed depths of less than a foot and a half. This was some mighty thin water for most boats, but *Fiddler* never touched bottom: the tide was high, the range of tide here being a little more than a foot, and the sailing was nearly downwind.

Once out of the lee of Parrott Island I picked up a little more speed as I approached the Whitestone Bridge, with its 110-foot vertical clearance, between Cherry Point and Grey Point. It looked as if Carter Creek, on the north shore just on the other side of the bridge, would be my haven for the night.

The river to the west looked much hazier now, and perhaps because of that, it appeared to be twice as wide and very much uninhabited. The weather looked threatening, which was unusual in light of the fact that there was little wind out of the northeast. I turned on my ten-dollar, cigarette-pack-sized Weatheradio from Radio Shack. The very first thing I heard was that the National Weather Service at Norfolk had issued a severe thunderstorm warning for the counties adjoining us. What did this mean?

I was reminded of Ecclesiastes: "He that increaseth knowledge increaseth sorrow." My friend Stan Sieja, who sailed around the world alone on a twenty-six-foot sloop, once told me about being asked by a fellow circumnavigator in the Fiji Islands about his electronics. Stan had proudly showed the questioner his flashlight, the only piece of electrical gadgetry he had on board. He had nothing, and nobody, to warn him about hurricanes, typhoons, or severe thunderstorms.

Nevertheless, I decided to head into Carter Creek, the first creek on the north shore, the home of the fancy Tides Inn, and a sure shelter from whatever was going to come my way. Besides, it was getting late in the day, and I hadn't been in Carter Creek for almost twenty years — not since the time when, after suffering through a horrendous thunderstorm at the mouth of the Rappahannock, I had sailed in to have dinner at the Tides Inn and was barred from the dining room until I borrowed a jacket from a busboy. My turtleneck had barely sufficed as a substitute for shirt and tie. Undoubtedly things had changed. For one thing, the Tides Inn now called itself "America's Elegant Resort by the Bay," and advertised in the *New Yorker*.

I was in a posh neighborhood now. The red roofs of the Tides Inn dominated the point between Carter Creek and its Eastern Branch, and many estates vied for importance along the waterfront. Carter Cove still had a number of workboats, and a few unpretentious watermen's cottages were still hanging on to their increasingly valuable turf, but you could see that it would be just a matter of time, and not a long time either, before the yachts replaced the workboats, and the estates replaced the cottages.

Carter Creek is so well protected from any weather that the only decision to be made was in which of the many branches to anchor: in the *Dovekie*, privacy was always an important concern. The wind was now merely a zephyr, and I took a leisurely look at the chart. I could opt for Yopps Cove, Church Prong, Dunton Cove, Sams Cove, or Bridge Cove. But at the headwaters of the creek, past the inn and its swimming pool, past its marina and the posh 127-foot motor yacht *Miss Ann* that the resort provides for its guests, and past its little sandy and nettle-screened beach, there was a cove with two feet of water called Dead and Bones, and I couldn't resist taking a look at it. I rolled up my sail and rowed the last few hundred yards into the cove, until my oar blades touched bottom. Only two houses, mostly hidden in trees, were visible in the distance. This was probably as much privacy as I would be able to get in this popular and fashionable area. I lowered the anchor and set it as well as I could by rowing backward. I could easily have set the anchor by hand, but the bottom was extremely muddy and the water too shallow to swim in.

Dead and Bones Cove ended near one of the tees of the inn's golf course. The only danger here would be getting hit by a stray golf ball, for the fairway hazard actually crossed the cove. But at this late hour most of the golfers probably were having their cocktails or at least were on their way off the course, for the sky looked truly menacing. I lowered the mast to lessen the chance of a lightning strike. Besides, I needed it to help support my back porch roof so that I could stay dry if it rained.

It didn't rain. The front came through after dinner, but there was no rain or thunderstorm associated with it, at least not in my cove. The skies cleared, and a fine breeze ruffled my anchorage.

By the failing light I looked at my Rappahannock River chart. Dead and Bones Cove was just one of many wonderful names sprinkled around the chart: there were also Senora, Mollusk, Milestone, Harry George Creek, Punchbowl Point, Upright, Welcome, and Water View—all places I would see again on the chart or visit in my boat in the days to come. I had come a little more than ten miles. Fredericksburg was a long way up the river.

The whine of a chainsaw woke me just after sunrise. A new pier was being built, and a new house was being squeezed into the already crowded waterfront. I was surprised not to find a breeze, after the frontal passage and the memory of the brisk breeze when I went to sleep. But this was Chesapeake Bay in midsummer, and almost anything was possible . . . and likely. The water in the cove looked gray, with myriads of nettles lazily propelling themselves just under the surface. It was time to look for other, perhaps even fresher, waters.

During breakfast I heard the whack of a golf club hitting its mark, and I saw, or imagined I saw, the little ball flying across the end of my cove. I now had even more motivation to get under way. I hastily cleaned the dishes, stowed the gear, and took down my tent. It took a while to recover the anchor, and I was glad to have had so little scope out in this shallow pool, for every inch of the line had hanging from it tentacles that were reluctant to let go and difficult to dislodge. With the mast still in its stowed position, I rowed out of the creek toward the river. It was about a mile to the entrance, and it took a little less than half an hour to cover that distance: I could never get *Fiddler* to move more quickly under oar power. Several watermen were working their crab pots in the creek (all wearing gloves), but none looked surprised at the white boat with the oars sticking out of the sides, and the head of the rower barely show-ing above the deck: they'd been watching the antics of the "come-heres" for years, and nothing surprised them anymore. And nobody seemed to be awake yet on any of the goldplater yachts I passed.

Because rowing *Fiddler* hid my body, doing so always brought thoughts of Greek and Roman galleys, and their galley slaves. Outboard motors have replaced slaves in the propulsion of dinghies. But sailors throughout history have not been particularly fond of oars. One of the oldest folktales, dating back to Homer, and found in many maritime cul-tures, concerns the man who walks away from the sea with an oar over his shoulder. When asked where he is going, he replies, "I am going to walk inland until I get to a place where people ask what this thing is."

Once past the creek's entrance, I cut the markers and headed across the shoals that make out from Orchard Point. Once in a while I could feel my oar blades hit the bottom ever so slightly. An older man with a beer belly stood at the edge of his lawn, watching me intently.

"You're out of the channel," he hollered, sounding indignant. I couldn't let go of the oars to acknowledge his observation with a thumbs-up signal, so I nodded my agreement. Somehow, perhaps through his body language, I got the idea that my running aground here would have given him huge satisfaction. It gave me great satisfaction to know that if I did run aground, I would merely have to step out of the boat, give it a little push in the direction of deeper water, and be on my way again.

Still, I was pleased to reach the river without hitting the bottom. And I wasn't going to row to Fredericksburg. Although there was no breeze in the river, I shipped the oars, raised the mast, and unfurled the sail. In less than a minute I had turned *Fiddler* from rowboat into sailboat. At first the sail was only good for shade, but after a while a bit of a breeze came up out of the southeast, dead aft. I wasn't going any faster now, but I was no longer working so hard.

I slowly coasted across the twin-branched mouth of the Corrotoman River. A quick glance at the chart showed dozens of potential anchorages for *Fiddler*. And the landscape was more beautiful, more pastoral, and less developed than the area around Carter Creek. But the fall line on the Rappahannock was a long way away, so I skipped the Corrotoman, as well as the next creek, Urbanna, on the south shore of the Rappahannock. The town of Urbanna, first proposed as a site for a port more than three hundred years ago, is a pleasant town, as I knew from previous visits.

A visitor in 1793 noted that

> Urbanna was formerly a place of some trade and importance; for as the customhouse for the Rappahannock was there, the vessels were obliged to clear at that port. But the customhouse being removed to Port Royal, it is now a deserted village and as the land in the neighborhood is engrossed by a few great proprietors there are only three or four store- or shopkeepers in the town, besides some sauntering young men, the vacuity of whose countenances unites with the grass-covered streets to give the place a most melancholy aspect. I believe there are not above a dozen houses in the town.

Two hundred years later, there was a big condominium complex at the entrance to the creek, and I decided to keep moving, propelled by what little wind I could catch.

Once I was past Urbanna, the Rappahannock River Bridge disappeared from sight. Not long after, the condos were hidden by Ball Point. A pastoral serenity settled on the river, where I kept company with two other sailboats, which were moving as slowly as *Fiddler*. Whatever had happened to those prevailing southwesterly breezes that dominate the weather in Virginia in the summer? "The sommer is hot as in Spaine," Captain Smith wrote. "The heat of sommer is in June, Julie, and August, but commonly the coole Breeses asswage the vehemencie of the heat."

There was little "assuaging" going on. The wind stayed light, and aft. The hottest part of the day was still hours away. I looked longingly at the water. The jellyfish were fewer in number, but larger. Sometimes, when the mainsheet dragged in the water, the slimy tentacles of the nettles would be wrapped around the rope as it lifted back in the air. Just before noon I hove to, waited until the boat drifted into a relatively nettle-free patch, and with a safety line in my hand took a very quick cooling dip into the river and scrambled back on board on the swim ladder I had hung from the gunwales. It cooled me off, and I wasn't stung, but there was a lot to be said for a self-draining cockpit in which one could just empty a bucket of (strained) seawater over one's head.

A mile or so further along, and a half hour later, I rounded up behind a pretty little beach at the entrance to Weeks Creek, ran *Fiddler* up on the beach, and made lunch. The tide was low, and just beginning to flood, and even if I had been able to find a spot of water free of nettles, the creek would still have been too shallow for any more swimming. But the creek was deserted, and the sky crystal-clear and cloudless, making a gorgeous setting for a picnic.

The wind picked up a bit after lunch, to around ten miles per hour, and so the air felt cooler. I skirted Stove Point and Smoky Point, and then edged around the Punchbowl, a narrow, shallow bay that got my vote as one of the most beautiful and secure spots in which to be when there was a hard gale from the northeast.

At McKans Bay the river was still several miles wide, and the scenery was very rural. The shore at McKans Bay is sixty to seventy feet high, and predictably, few houses had been built there, since not too many people would be willing to build a six- or seven-story-high flight of steps to get down to their pier.

But the blank stretch of horizon was getting smaller as the river narrowed near the old lighthouse foundation at Bowlers Wharf. I headed for the northern shore and the entrance to Totuskey Creek. Just before Totuskey, a smaller creek, called Richardson, came into view, and looked more inviting and more secure for an anchorage. The chart said two feet; I felt my way in and anchored in five feet. I stared at the water surrounding the boat for a full five minutes, but saw no nettles. For the next half hour I splashed around in the cool, almost fresh water, cleaning *Fiddler's* hull in between laps around the boat.

Near the end of the afternoon a fast and fancy motorboat came roaring up the creek, throwing a humongous wake. It continued on for another few hundred yards, and then, running into shoal water, slowed down and turned back toward my anchorage.

"What creek is this?" demanded its skipper without a greeting or preamble. I told him, and he roared off without another word, leaving me rocking and rolling in his wake. Stinkpotters! I'll never understand them.

The drainage basin of the Rappahannock River takes in nearly three thousand square miles of land, roughly two-thirds of which is forested, most of the rest being covered in crops and pasture. Only a tiny 2 percent of the land use in the basin is urban, and so most of the area has remained unspoiled and rural. Between the fall line and the Chesapeake, the Rappahannock's bounty provides commercial fishermen with an industry valued at more than $4 million per year. Endangered species also value the area: in 1992, researchers from the College of William and Mary found 127 active American bald eagle nests in Virginia. Nearly one-third, 41, were found on the Rappahannock, although the Potomac, with 37 nests, ran a close second. It is unimaginable but true that during the Civil War Virginia paid a bounty to those who killed bald eagles, since the bird represented the Union forces.

There are more than thirteen thousand acres of wetlands along the shores of the river, but few settlements. Tappahannock, about halfway up the tidal portion of the river, is the largest one. That's where I was headed.

The water in Richardson Creek might have been fresh enough to discourage the sea nettles, but there was apparently enough salt in it that the blue crab still scavenged this far up the river, for in the morning the two pots I'd hung overboard came up looking immaculate. At dawn it seemed that several hours would pass before any wind would arrive, and I promptly dirtied one of the two pans again with the makings of an elaborate breakfast.

About once a week I departed from my standard breakfast routine. My usual breakfast consisted of a bowl of cornflakes with as much fruit as I could lay my hands on, over which I poured orange juice. This habit had struck many people as disgusting and possibly insane, but the discovery of the pleasure of this concoction was so momentous that I easily remember the date and place: April 1983, in Fort Lauderdale, Florida. I had been a weekend guest aboard a large sailboat skippered by my friend Captain Thomas Kidd. At daybreak I found Tom laying out the makings of breakfast: cornflakes, fresh fruit, orange juice, and coffee. When I asked about milk for the cereal, Tom said that he never used it: had I ever tried orange juice? I thought he was joking. But he wasn't, and I reluctantly tried the combination. I haven't had any milk in my cereal since. It changed my life. Well, it changed my breakfast habits. And properly packaged orange juice (if real oranges were not available) didn't have to be refrigerated.

In any case, this morning I broke the fast with poached eggs, corned beef hash, toast, and coffee. I cleaned the pot myself, since I couldn't wait for the crabs to do their excellent but time-consuming work. Besides, several crabbers near my anchorage were doing their best to catch my scullery helpers.

A tiny breeze sprang up while I was cleaning the dishes. By eight I was under way, making perhaps a half mile per hour. By nine I had doubled my speed. Tappahannock was five miles—five hours at this rate—up the river. I was disinclined to row, for I kept hoping that the breeze would pick up any minute. Besides, I was in no hurry.

The only things that marred the landscape were the power lines across the river between Wares Wharf and Accaceek Point. Farms bordered the river's north shore. Houses were few. After a time, the last stretch of unobstructed horizon turned into the outline of the bridge at Tappahannock.

By late morning I had reached a point called Mangoright, where I decided to go left. I secured my sail, started the engine, and plowed a wake across the placid river to Hoskins Creek, the tiny harbor of Tappahannock.

Tappahannock, whose name is a variant of Rappahannock, an Indian name thought to mean "Place of Tidal Waters," was called Hobses Hole until 1680, when the site was selected for one of twenty new towns in Virginia and became known as New Plymouth. The name was changed to Tappahannock in 1706.

In 1774 Philip Fithian, a young tutor at the home of Colonel Carter, wrote, "This is a small village, with only a few Stores and Shops; it is on a beautiful River, and has, I am told, six, eight and ten Ships loading before it." A hundred and fifty years later, Dora Chinn Jett wrote *In Tidewater Virginia,* from which comes this effusive sentence: "Tappahannock! there is a certain poetic quality in the assembled syllables, apart from the significance of the word, something picturesque, and suggestive of wigwams, wampum, mulberry, and locust trees! also tomahawks, arrowheads, and pow-wows!"

I saw nothing of the sort. Just inside Hoskins Creek I found the remains of a marina. A crudely lettered sign announced that I was at the Admirals Club. In front of a barely upright building were five slips, three of which were occupied by small sailboats. I scooted into an empty slip and looked around for signs of life. The doors to the building were open, but the building was deserted. I decided to go for a walk along the pretty, tree-lined streets. The tiny downtown area of Tappahannock had been spruced up, and the three mercantile ventures most important to cruisers—grocery store, hardware store, and bookstore—were within a few blocks of the water. I tried to participate in the local economy by buying things at all three stores, but was only successful at the hardware store, where I bought two spark plugs (I hadn't changed the plugs in years). The "convenience" grocery store inconveniently didn't have any fresh fruit, and the bookstore appeared to sell only gothic romances and used comic books. I asked the proprietor about books about the Rappahannock River.

"Oh, I can't keep them in stock," she lamented.

"What about a book called *Five Fair Rivers?*" I asked, always prepared to do market research.

"It goes as fast as it comes in," she said. I was immensely reassured.

I continued my walk through the town for half an hour more and then returned to the "marina," but not without having discovered a new condominium on the riverfront—just like the one at Urbanna. There was still no sign of life at the Admirals Club, and I ate my lunch on the falling-down wharf. At one o'clock I motored back out into the river, looking for wind. I found some, but there was barely enough of it to propel me up the river. Most of the progress that I made was by way of the current.

Once under the Tappahannock bridge I noticed that the crab pots had disappeared. And as I stared at the water, I also noticed that the nettles were no longer in evidence. I leaned over the gunwale and tasted the water. I could not detect a trace of salt, although the official dividing line between salt and fresh water would not come for another ten miles or so, near Leedsville. The most beloved and the most despised creatures of the Chesapeake would not figure in the rest of my journey up the Rappahannock.

I headed for Mallorys Point, disdaining the channel. By cutting off some bends in the river, and cutting across shoals, I probably shortened my route by 10 percent, and incidentally also made the sailing more interesting. And at Mallorys Point the first of the truly abrupt turns in the river began, and the river vistas changed dramatically. The enormous houses lining the river's bank west of Tappahannock were left behind, and marshes began to dominate the scenery. My progress was slow, but why would I want to hurry through this landscape?

It remained stiflingly hot until the middle of the afternoon, when, mercifully, the sky clouded over, the sun disappeared, and a fresh breeze — which was, miraculously, favorable — sprang up. About eight miles above Tappahannock, high cliffs began to appear on the north shore. These are part of the same geologic formation as the Nomini, Stratford, and Horsehead Cliffs, on the south shore of the Potomac, only seven miles away as the crow flies.

The river here, still very deep (the chart showed fifty-one feet), was now only a quarter of a mile wide. With the breeze behind me, and the current helping out, it didn't take long to pass the several miles of hundred-foot-high cliffs, but I didn't want to let them out of my sight. At a bend in the river which the chart showed as Thomas Neck, I headed for the marshes, and shallower water, opposite the last of the cliffs. When the hinged rudder touched bottom, at two and a half feet, I lowered the anchor and furled the sail. I was protected from the breeze, partially surrounded by marshes, in a landscape without a manmade thing in sight. It was six o'clock, and I would have another three hours of daylight to enjoy this marvelous scenery. I let out anchor line until *Fiddler* drifted back into six feet of water, and then I went for a long, refreshing swim.

I'd covered about twenty miles, despite light winds, a lengthy walk, and for the most part, contrary current. In the morning I would have a favoring current again. The wind would be out of the south, but from here on, the wind direction wouldn't matter much, for around the next bend the Rappahannock, like the James, would begin her "curles," and I would be moving south and east almost as often as I'd move north and west.

Just before midnight I awoke to a violent rolling motion, if a flat-bottomed boat can be said to roll. Clouds had moved in, and the stars were no longer visible. The current had switched and set up a surge against the fresh breeze up the river, the surge reaching around my little arm of marsh. I hadn't tucked myself in far enough.

Reluctantly I got out of my sleeping bag, raised the anchor, and, grateful for the convenience, started the motor and moved further into the little bay, my flashlight barely outlining the edge of the marsh. A few hundred yards later the waters were quieter. I reanchored. *Fiddler* was motionless, and I was soon sound asleep once more.

At dawn I realized that my nighttime doings had actually put me in an even prettier spot. The cliffs and the river, now lit by the morning sun, still looked dazzling in the distance, but I was now nestled in a little gut of the marsh, surrounded by blooming arrowhead and pickerel weed. The moon, in its last quarter, was still visible above the cliffs. Although the water was calm in my anchorage, I saw ripples on the river in the distance. By seven I had finished the chores and made sail, and was under way. The wind waned before it had a chance to wax. Still, it lasted long enough to move me to the next hard turn in the river. Some miles earlier, I had spotted what I thought was a white sail, and I eagerly looked forward to "speaking" another vessel. The triangular patch turned out to be the gable end of a small cottage. When I'd completely run out of wind, I rowed; then I sailed again when a barely perceptible breeze returned in late morning. My progress was maddeningly slow, but my stately pace was not without pleasure, for the scenery was spectacular. At one bold turn in the river I sailed past Wheatland, a handsome Federal-style farmhouse, and Saunders Wharf, the only steamboat landing remaining on the Rappahannock.

After Ketch Point and Blind Point there came another straight stretch of water, and imposing cliffs appeared again near Horsehead Point — which I could by no stretch of the imagination visualize as a part of an animal. I had seen no one on the river all morning, but I was rewarded by the sight of three bald eagles lofting above the cliffs. A few houses began to appear near Portobago Bay, a small, shallow hump in the river a few miles from Port Royal. Before civilization became too apparent, I decided to anchor for lunch and a swim. I didn't bother to furl the sail, since there was no air in evidence. After a long swim and a cucumber sandwich I continued my drift up the river at something like a quarter of a mile per hour.

Portobago Bay, tree-lined all around, but also tree-littered, obstructed by trunks lying in the shallow water, offered a little more wind, but it still took nearly two hours to reach the bridge at Port Royal — and I rowed the last mile. I arrived at the decrepit (and only) pier in Port Royal with blisters on my derrière. I had seldom experienced such a fickle, mostly windless day. The air became more humid, the cumulus clouds grew larger, and the river in the distance beyond the bridge grew more hazy. I had twenty-five miles more to go to reach Fredericksburg, but I knew that there would be no facilities further up the river, and I needed to make arrangements by telephone to be retrieved later in the week. I also yearned for a cold beer. I tied *Fiddler* to a swaying pole at the end of the rickety pier (which a tourist brochure grandly described as Port Royal Landing) and allowed her to drift away from it in the current, and I then went ashore, needing to cross a private yard to do so.

Port Royal is a great place if you need fireworks. Route 301, the main road through the tiny town, is a busy truck route, and both sides of the road have a number of stands selling fireworks (which are legal in Virginia). But if you come by water, and you need fuel, or groceries, or even drinking water, it's a long, scary walk to a store: there are no sidewalks. I found a telephone after a long hike in the hot sun, and bought some cold beer. By the time I got back to my boat, the beer was almost warm again.

Port Royal was created in 1744 by an act of the Virginia assembly. A sixty-acre plan was adopted for a site along the river. In 1775 a visitor noted that the river at this point was "A little more than a quarter of a Mile across, but deep enough to carry Vessels of great Burthen." The town then contained "20 or 30 dwelling houses, & about 6 stores, all Scotch." When river traffic declined, Port Royal turned its back to the river, making the highway its economic focal point. I made my way back down to the water, boarded *Fiddler,* and rowed under the new, stationary bridge, which had replaced an old swing bridge a few years earlier. Another mile upriver I met the first vessel I'd seen all day—vessels, rather, for they were tugboat and barge. All hands waved at the galley slave in the strange-looking boat. Even the cook, dressed in shorts, came out of his galley and made a thumbs-up sign.

After a mile of oarsmanship, I cranked up the engine. With the bridge out of sight, there were no more artificial intrusions on the lovely landscape except for a small sign, nearly hidden away in some low brush, that read, "Please Do Not Fish Near Here. Your Motors Disturb the Peace. Thank You for Your Understanding." There wasn't a house in sight, but I promptly shut my engine down and resumed rowing. I had about a half mile to go toward Goat Island, a marshy clump on a sharp bend, where I hoped to find a quiet and sheltered anchorage. It was too hot to go on much longer, and thunderstorms later in the afternoon seemed a safe bet. At four I dropped the hook in five feet of water in the Thorofare, a spectacularly lovely anchorage off the river, which cut a half mile or so off the river's length and made Goat Island an island.

Naturally, no sooner had I straightened things out on the boat and taken a quick swim than a light breeze sprang up. But enough was enough: it had been a fiercely hot and humid day, and I had walked and rowed for many hours. It was time to relax in this Eden. Whichever direction the wind blew from, I'd have plenty of protection.

After dinner I heard a lot of rumbling. Low, dark clouds alternated with ballooning cumulus clouds. Just before dark a hefty, cool breeze came up out of the east. I lowered the mast, tented myself in, and waited for the rain.

Wispy, smoky fog hung a few feet above the river's surface when I awoke the next morning. Lightning had awakened me at three, and I had watched the fireworks spectacle for half an hour before falling asleep again. There had been little rain, and no squalls, but a cold front had surely passed. The air felt cool and clean. I slept later than usual and lingered over breakfast, then read and puttered around the boat.

A little after seven, the sun appeared over the trees and began to dry my canvas. But still there was no breeze. It looked as if rowing would be the order of the day once more. I had about fifteen miles to go to Fredericksburg, where I had arranged to be met with *Fiddler's* trailer on the following day. It was difficult to measure the distance accurately on the chart because of the twists and turns of the river. But the trip certainly would take most of the day. When the canvas had dried, I rolled up the dodger and stowed the tent. I recovered the anchor, opened the rowing ports, slid the ten-foot oars through, and rowed up the Thorofare to rejoin the river.

The oar blades kept hitting the bottom. I could find no obvious deep channel, although mudbanks were in evidence in some of the straight stretches. It was a struggle, but by nine I was out of the maze and back in the Rappahannock River. I might have saved some distance, but I certainly hadn't saved any time. As I came out of the narrow gut I nearly plowed into a fisherman in a small skiff. I don't know who was more surprised.

"How'd you get through there?" he asked, pointing at the nearly invisible opening from which I had just emerged. "How much do you draw? There's no water in there!"

I held up four fingers.

"There's no four feet in there even at high tide!"

I held up my four fingers again. "Four inches," I allowed. I didn't say anything about having had to get out and haul *Fiddler* across two of the mudbanks.

"You came all the way through the Thorofare? That's amazing!" He kept looking at my boat, mast down, oars sticking out, only my head visible above the deck. "Where are you headed?" I told him. He kept shaking his head in disbelief.

"If I get any kind of breeze I'll be there tonight," I said, and started rowing again.

"If I can get this damn motor started I could be there in half an hour," he said. "I'm gonna wait till the tide comes up, though."

I had made my transit of the Thorofare at low tide! I had calculated the tidal stage on the basis of information for Hampton Roads. But this far up the Rappahannock, tidal predictions were based on data for Washington, D.C., and the Potomac River, only a dozen miles to the north. If I had paid more attention to clues in my surroundings, such as watermarks on the flora along the banks, I would have figured it out, but in that case I probably would have avoided the Thorofare and thus would have missed an interesting and beautiful alternate route.

A half mile past Goat Island a breeze came up, and I gratefully raised the mast and began to sail. But the winds teased all day. For ten minutes I'd get a decent tack under my belt, and then—nothing. When there was no wind, I could feel the cool of the earlier morning fast disappearing. I left the mast up when I rowed and the oars sticking out when I sailed. Several times I jumped into the river, holding on to the mainsheet. But the river was beautiful, and I had the place to myself. Sometimes I would be headed south and east, instead of north and west, my destination. For several hundred years, until the advent of the steam engine, mariners had made their way up and down these rivers this way, using sail and oars, winds and tides.

All the reaches and bends had names, and you can bet that apprentice seamen in the eighteenth and nineteenth centuries had to learn them by heart. From Tappahannock to Fredericksburg there were dozens of them: Mangoright, Layton Reach, Devils Reach, Devils Elbow, North Bend, Mud Folly Bend, Carter Short Turn, Mount Reach, Egghouse Reach, Lagrange Turn, Hollywood Bend, Buckners Reach, Slipe Reach, Morelan Reach, Springhill Reach, Rock Creek Turn, Park Turn, Longrange Turn, Popcastle Turn, Devils Woodyard Turn, Farleyvale Reach, Fox Spring Bend, Epson Turn, and Dangerfield Short Turn.

Late in the morning the current became favorable, and my progress was a bit better. But I wasn't really complaining. The slow progress allowed a closer look at the splendid scenery along the riverbanks. At noon I ran the boat up on a sandbank along the river's edge, made a chicken salad for lunch, and drank a beer. The salad was canned, and the beer was warm, but I didn't mind. In another day or so I would be driving at sixty-five miles per hour on some interstate, watching thunderstorms glow red on Doppler radar on television, and enjoying hot showers and cold beers. Greater contrast was hard to imagine.

The lack of good wind somehow contributed to my sense of serenity. I didn't have to constantly focus my attention on the boat. I didn't mind moving slowly, for that left lots of time to contemplate my surroundings. Even though there were few signs of civilization—a house once in a while, a buoy at some turn in the river—the river was much as it had been four hundred years ago. It was then undoubtedly deeper, with fewer shoals. The trees would have been significantly larger in the seventeenth century, the fish more abundant (although they were jumping out of the water all around me), the wildlife more varied, and the water cleaner (although it was now certainly safe to swim in).

The Rappahannock, like all rivers in America, has its share of problems. A dozen years ago, a ruptured oil pipeline dumped nearly one hundred thousand gallons of petroleum products into the Rapidan (a tributary of the Rappahannock), which rendered the drinking-water supply of Fredericksburg unfit for use for more than a week. Until recently, trash was routinely dumped into the river. Since about one-third of the land in the Rappahannock basin is used for agriculture, much pollution in the river comes from the runoff from farms, which can include pesticides, manures, soil, and fertilizers.

The U.S. Soil Conservation Service estimates that fifteen tons of soil per acre washes off the rolling hills in the upper Rappahannock basin each year—more than twice the amount that soil scientists consider acceptable. It all ends up in the river, and much of it eventually makes its way to the Chesapeake. In the meantime, the soil clouds the water, smothering plants and fish eggs, and even clogging the gills of mature fish with sediment. Manure carries bacteria, often making shellfish un-harvestable and creating health hazards for humans, while pesticides and herbicides can be toxic to all forms of life. Fertilizers loaded with nitrogen and phosphorus create problems, as do discharges from sewage treatment plants and industrial plants. One of the major problems in dealing with these insults to the river is that the villains are mostly invisible — and the river still looks so beautiful.

Although the day was almost a carbon copy of the day before, hot and humid, after noon the wind picked up, and held. The wind on a river tends to follow the river's course, upriver — or down. In my experience it almost always blows against the sailor's intended course, and on my penultimate day on the Rappahannock I spent a good portion of the afternoon tacking against the wind. The flood current abated in mid-afternoon and turned against me soon after. At five I decided to stop. I was about five miles from Fredericksburg, and still only one house was vaguely visible through the trees about a mile away. I anchored in about eight feet of water just off the channel. I was out of current, out of wind, nearly out of gas, and out of steam. But the anchorage was serene, the swimming refreshing, and the solitude absolute until the fisherman I'd met earlier in the day raced by at a wakeless, planing, thirty-odd miles per hour. We waved. It had been a long day for him, too, and if he'd caught any fish he would still have to clean them. I opened a can of salmon and started my dinner.

It was slowly getting lighter. I raised my head from the sleeping bag to look through the rowing port. It *was* lighter outside than in my tented shelter, but I couldn't see anything. I slid the main standing-room hatch open and was momentarily disoriented. *Fiddler* seemed to be afloat in a sphere of gray, and moving, but in what direction I could not tell. Then I realized that what was moving was the river — we were still firmly an-chored to its bottom — and that the motion was the only thing that gave me a clue which way my destination lay: the tide was ebbing. I couldn't see the edge of the river, which I knew to be less than one hundred feet away to port. I had seldom seen fog so thick.

I opened up my tent, got dressed, and started to make breakfast. It would be a while before I could get under way. It had occurred to me that lack of wind, or an opposing current, or a failed engine might keep me from my rendezvous in Fredericksburg, but the possibility of a heavy fog had never crossed my mind. It was too dangerous to proceed, I thought, not because of the route, which could hardly lead me astray, but because of other traffic. After all, it was Saturday morning, and fishing skiffs might be headed out, at flank speed, to look for catfish, carp, crappies, or, more likely at this time of year, largemouth and smallmouth bass. I decided to wait until visibility was a quarter mile or better before venturing forth.

As the morning advanced, the outline of the sun was revealed through a stand of trees on the near shore. As the air warmed, the fog evaporated. A half hour later, the first of the fishermen roared by. It was time to go to town.

Fredericksburg was named after Frederick Louis, Prince of Wales and the eldest son of King George II. The town was laid out in 1727. In 1732 George Washington's father, who owned "Ferry Farm," across the Rappahannock, bought three lots in the town and became one of the town's trustees. The town was incorporated in 1781. It was among the busiest seaports in colonial America, and as ocean-going ships became too large to make their way to the city's wharves, Fredericksburg developed into a regional center of commerce. At the beginning of the Civil War, five thousand people were living in the town, where in December 1862 some of the bloodiest battles of the war were to take place, involving two hundred thousand troops and resulting in eighteen thousand casualties. During the heavy fighting the city changed hands seven times, its chamber of commerce is fond of pointing out, although how that could be ascertained in the chaos and confusion of the battle is hard to understand.

There was no wind, at least not yet, but I raised the mast and

set sail anyway. This was part hope and part vigilance, for *Fiddler*'s tanbark sail would make her more visible in the remaining patches of fog.
I rowed for a mile, and when the tide turned, later in the morning, I
coasted with the current, occasionally feeling a small boost to the boat's
speed as the wind began to ruffle the water and smooth the sail. I passed
a few abandoned wharves near Sylvania Heights, where decades ago the
Sylvania Industrial Corporation had a plant. The cavalier attitude toward
the river at that time was revealed in some navigational advice in the
1937 *Coast Pilot:* "The river pilot reports in 1935 that during ordinary
weather he regularly takes acid barges drawing 11½ feet up the river
to the Sylvania plant, but pushes through mud on several of the bars in
doing so."

I knew that I was taking each turn more slowly than the one before,
preparing myself for the end of this lovely, quiet cruise. After the last
marker on the river, number 135, a mile from the city, a golf course came
into view, and then some houses, a few small piers, and a telephone relay
tower. I met more outbound fishing boats. Still, I could have anchored in
complete privacy a half mile from Fredericksburg. The trees came down
to the water's edge, and the river was now less than five hundred feet
wide. Then the first of the bridges appeared. A launching ramp at a small
riverside park was swarming with bass boats and trailers. I bagged my
sail, lowered the mast, and when the last of the fishermen had sped off,
headed for the ramp and *Fiddler*'s waiting trailer.

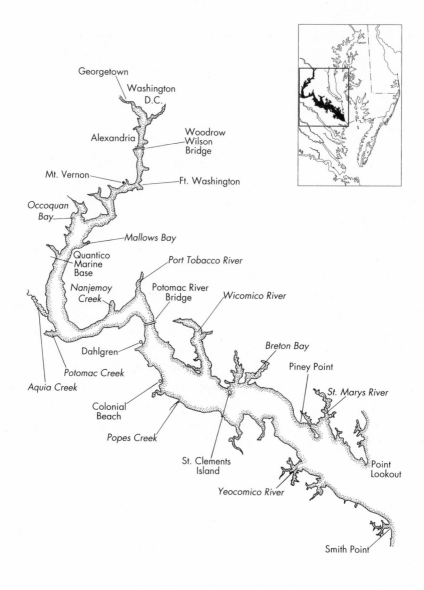

Georgetown

Washington
D.C.

Woodrow
Wilson
Bridge

Alexandria

Mt. Vernon

Ft. Washington

Occoquan
Bay

Mallows Bay

Quantico
Marine
Base

Port Tobacco River

Nanjemoy
Creek

Potomac River
Bridge

Wicomico River

Dahlgren

Breton Bay

Piney Point

Potomac Creek

St. Marys River

Aquia Creek

Colonial
Beach

Popes Creek

St. Clements
Island

Point
Lookout

Yeocomico River

Smith Point

The Potomac

The Potomac River and its beauty may be truly known only by those who sail from the head of tidewater along the winding reaches, into every estuary to the Bay. . . . A slow cruise in a slow cruising sailboat is an absolute requirement.

—Frederick Tilp, *This Was Potomac River,* 1978

The Potomac of to-day can be truly known only by the pilgrim who steers his boat into the broad mouth and rides the whole course of the tide until the force of the "ffreshes" halts him.

—Paul Wilstach, *Potomac Landings,* 1932

It is a remarkable fact that the English have been given credit for being the first explorers of the Chesapeake—and of the Potomac. In 1588, two decades before Captain John Smith's "discovery" of the Potomac, Capitán Vicente Gonzales sailed northward from Saint Augustine, in Florida, and entered the Bahia de Madre de Dios. It was his second trip into the Chesapeake: it was he who had delivered some ill-fated Jesuit missionaries to the James River in 1570. A bare-bones description of the Potomac has survived:

As they continued to sail north, the land from the east jutted into the bay. . . . They discovered inlets and coves as well as rivers along the western shore. Then they came upon a large fresh-water river, which, where it entered the bay, was more than 6 fathoms deep. To the north there was very high land, with ravines, but without trees, delightful and free, which has the aspect of a green field and was pleasant to behold. On the south shore of this river the beach is very calm and is lined with small pebbles. Farther up the south bank of the same river there appeared a delightful valley, wooded, and pleasant land which seemed to be fertile and adaptable to stock-raising and farming. The river was located in a latitude of 38°. They named it San Pedro.

Native Americans, of course, had been wandering the river's edge for thousands of years, hunting, fishing, and raising tobacco, beans, and corn. The tribes were of Algonquin stock "and of a peaceful nature." Their settlements were confined to the shores of the Potomac and its tributaries. On what came to be known as the Virginia side of the river were tribes of the Powhatan Confederacy, and on the side soon to be called Maryland were Piscataways, Nanticokes, Potopacos, Nacostines, and others.

"The fourth river," Captain Smith wrote of his "5. faire . . . rivers," "is called Patawomeke and is 6 or 7 miles in breadth. It is navigable 140 miles, and fed as the rest with many sweet rivers and springs, which fall from the bordering hils. These hils many of them are planted, and yeelde no lesse plenty and variety of fruit than the river exceedeth with abundance of fish. This river is inhabited on both sides."

He had reason to know. Smith had spent a month on the Potomac in 1608, during the first of his two "voyages of discovery," searching for gold and that always elusive passage to China. This was more time than he spent on any other river but the James. Yet in the *Proceedings of the English Colony* he writes fewer than five hundred words about the adventure that he undertook with fourteen other men in an open barge, during what came to be known as the "First Chesapeake Voyage":

> The 16 of June, we fel with the river of Patawomeck. Feare being gon, and our men recovered, wee were all contente to take some paines to knowe the name of this 9 mile broad river. We could see no inhabitants for 30 myles saile. Then we were conducted by 2 Salvages up a little bayed creeke toward Onawmament, where all the woods were laid with Ambuscadoes to the number of 3 or 400 Sal-

vages, but so strangely painted, grimed, and disguised, showting, yelling, and crying, as we rather supposed them so many divels. They made many bravadoes, but to appease their furie, our Captaine prepared (with a seeming willingnesse, as they) to encounter them. The grazing of the bullets upon the river, with the ecco of the woods so amazed them, as down went their bowes and arrowes; and exchanging hostage, James Watkins was sent 6. myles up the woods, to their kings habitation. Wee were kindly used by these Salvages, of whom we understood, they were commaunded to betray us, by Powhatans direction, and hee so directed from the discontents of James towne. The like incounters we found at Patawomeck, Cecocawone, and divers other places; but at Moyaones, Nacothtant, and Taux, the people did their best to content us. The cause of this discovery was to search a glistering mettal, the Salvages told us they had from Patawomeck (the which Newport assured that he had tryed to hold halfe silver), also to search what furres, metals, rivers, Rockes, nations, woods, fishings, fruits, victuals, and other commodities the land afforded, and whether the bay were endlesse, or how farre it extended. The mine we found 9 or 10 myles up in the country from the river, but it proved of no value. Some Otters, Beavers, Martins, . . . and sables we found and, in diverse places, that abundance of fish lying so thicke with their heads above the water, as for want of nets (our barge driving amongst them) we attempted to catch them with a frying pan; but we found it a bad instrument to catch fish with. Neither better fish, more plenty or variety, had any of us ever seene in any place, swimming in the water, then in the bay of Chesapeack, but there not to be caught with frying-pans. To expresse al our quarrels, treacheries and incounters amongst those Salvages, I should be too tedious; but in briefe, at al times we so incountered them and curbed their insolencies, as they concluded with presents to purchase peace, yet wee lost not a man. At our first meeting, our captaine ever observed this order, to demaunde their bowes and arrowes, swords, mantles, or furres, with some childe for hostage: whereby he could quickly perceive when they intended any villany.

The Potomac River flows into the Chesapeake Bay seventy miles above the Virginia capes. The river is the boundary between Virginia on the west and Maryland on the east, but the boundary does not run down the middle: Maryland owns the Potomac. The head of navigation is at Chain Bridge, in Washington, D.C., more than one hundred miles from the river's mouth. That's where I was headed when I launched *Fiddler* late one morning in early September from a deserted ramp at Lake Conoy, part of Point Lookout State Park, on the northern side of the mouth of the imposing river.

The mouth of the Potomac, when measured from Point Lookout to Smith Point, is ten nautical miles wide. Even when measured from Point Lookout to the nearest point across, it is five miles wide—wider than the Chesapeake itself at its narrowest. It is a patch of open water to be reckoned with. One circumnavigator related that he'd been pooped— that is, he took a breaking wave over the stern—only twice in decades of ocean sailing: once off Tasmania, and once off the mouth of the Potomac.

Most cruising sailors would never consider Lake Conoy for an anchorage. Even the largest-scale charts show but a minuscule pond, and an entrance suitable for a dinghy, perhaps, but not for a yacht. Yet the entrance is marked by buoys, the channel itself carries depths of six feet, and the lake itself is uncommonly pretty. Overnight anchorage, however, except in emergencies, is not allowed; as a result, few cruising sailors experience the lake's solitude. The entrance to the lake was cut through in the 1970s. Before that time, vessels seeking shelter, especially from a nor'easter, rode out the weather in Cornfield Harbor, the bight just inside Point Lookout.

With a light easterly wind behind her, *Fiddler* had no trouble sailing out of Lake Conoy into Cornfield Harbor, and thence into the wide Potomac, bound for the fall line. I could just barely see the opposite shore. The Smith Point lighthouse, across the river, was below the horizon, but I could see the old, unused Point Lookout lighthouse sticking up above the scrub pine a half mile to the north. The lighthouse was built in 1830, and several women were numbered among its keepers.

One of the first, Ann Davis, was complimented in a report made in 1840 by the captain of the lighthouse service supply boat. "Mrs. Davis is a fine woman," he wrote, "and I am sorry she has to live on a small naked point of land." In the following decades the "naked point of land" became a popular summer resort, with a hotel and nearly a hundred cottages, but early in the Civil War it was leased by the U.S. government, and an army hospital was constructed on it. After the Battle of Gettysburg in 1863, a prison camp was built. The notorious Point Lookout prisoner of war camp held both Confederate soldiers and southern Maryland civilians accused of helping the Confederacy. By the summer of 1864, more than twenty thousand prisoners crowded the camp. Soon after the Civil War ended in April 1865, the last prisoners were released and the camp closed. Nearly thirty-five hundred had died. More than fifty thousand men (among them the poet Sidney Lanier, who spent four months at Point Lookout) had been imprisoned under the most wretched conditions.

One of these, John R. King, recounted his experiences in a book he published after the war. King spent the last year of the Civil War at the Point Lookout camp. His book is filled with stories of disease, degradation, and discomfort. Only one paragraph referred to the Potomac River, and it is one of the few not concerned with the hardships of the camp.

> The prison at Point Lookout was located on a narrow piece of ground about one quarter of a mile wide at the mouth of the Potomac River.... Bathing in the bay was a source of pleasure granted us.... It was a great relief to stand on the beach and watch ships and small craft pass.... Some with a line and a net waded in the water waist deep and caught the big crabs.

Point Lookout today is a state park; the prison is gone, and the lighthouse is the residence of the park's superintendent.

People were still fishing for crabs from the jetties flanking the narrow inlet, but there were no other boats in sight. The shore beyond the jetties consisted of pristine, sandy beaches. I headed due east across the shoals toward Cornfield Point, intending to follow the Maryland shore, at least for the first day or so. The first large anchorage on the south shore of the Potomac lies in the Coan River, a dozen miles upriver from Smith Point, although *Fiddler,* with her four-inch draft, could perhaps have made it into several of the three or four marshy guts in between. I decided, however, to try, while the wind was favorable, to gain some distance upriver. And so I missed the first creeks on the Virginia side, the Coan and Yeocomico Rivers, both with more tentacled branches than some of the jellyfish I was starting to see.

The day was sunny and bright, but humid, and the possibility of thunderstorms later in the day concerned me. Although the Dovekie could find shelter nearly anywhere, the sheer size of the Potomac at its mouth was imposing. As I skirted the edge of Cornfield Harbor and the breeze crept up to ten knots, *Fiddler* began making pleasant little noises. I fancied that she was glad to be back on another river and was showing it by making slapping, watery sounds.

It is always pleasant to start a cruise with the wind behind; it gets things started without being too hectic. And if the temperature is in the low eighties, and the current a bit favorable, few things in life can compare with being on a small sailboat on a river voyage. "The most difficult thing about sailing a Dovekie," I once wrote in *The Shallow Water Sailor,* a newsletter for folks interested in boats that can float on a heavy dew, "is wrestling the tiller out of my wife's hand." I was sailing alone on these mini-voyages, and the only thing I now regretted was that— because a Dovekie cannot be left alone for a moment if you hope to keep her moving—I was unable to sit in my favorite seat on the Dovekie: in the hatch on the bow. Self-steering is not an option.

I completely forgot about lunch. I nibbled on some raisins and sipped some seltzer, but I was intimidated by the distance I had ahead of me—one hundred miles—and I wanted to make a good start. "At sea," Nigel Calder once wrote, "you should not say you are going 'to' somewhere, because who knows what wind and weather will do? 'Towards' avoids hubris." I headed "towards" the District of Columbia.

I gurgled along, a hundred feet off the beaches, dodging fish weirs. Along a few stretches there were summer cottages, some boarded up, and here and there more pretentious homes. A man in yellow pajamas ran out of one of the cottages and trained his binoculars on *Fiddler*. I waved, but he didn't return the greeting. After a while he ran back into his house. I guessed that he'd been trying to decide whether we posed a threat; or perhaps he'd never before seen anyone sail so close to the edge of the river.

I had wanted to go up the Saint Marys River to the fabulous anchorage called Horseshoe Bend, where the Maryland colonists settled in 1634. But the breeze backed into the northeast and I would have to beat to windward to get there, something I didn't want to do on my first day on the river.

And I wasn't making much progress. I had no way to tell, but I felt that I was bucking a slight current. Sailors, of course, always tell themselves (or their crew) that the current is at fault if progress is not as swift as expected. So I decided to sail parallel to the shore, skip Smith Creek and the Saint Marys River, and duck into Saint George Creek, the narrow ribbon that separates Saint George Island and Piney Point from the river. The creek is not much used, at least by sailboats, for there is a fixed bridge with a clearance of only seventeen feet which prevents reentering the Potomac at the other end. But I could lower my boat's mast and thus would not have to backtrack.

A good-sized yacht came out of the Saint Marys River, furiously motoring toward the Chesapeake. I could see four other boats, all under sail, in the distance at various points of the compass. The horizon ahead and behind was unburdened by land. I had heard earlier on my little weather radio that the front that was expected to clear the weather up had become stationary, and that another day or two of humid weather was in the offing. But that meant that the wind would give me a reach or a run. My destination lay to the northwest—the direction from which the wind would come after a cold front passed. My fall cruise was not yet a cool one.

Storm clouds, though, were making up in the northwest. It would be many hours before they would affect me, for thunderstorms on the Chesapeake seldom come up before four in the afternoon. In a thunderstorm a Dovekie, like any other boat, is best handled by anchoring in as protected a place as can be found. I picked out a likely spot, Price Cove, off Saint George Creek, to spend the night. If I couldn't make that anchorage in time, I could always run back into Smith Creek. I felt ambivalent about the weather forecasts, which were no more than predictions. If one waited for all the proper circumstances and conditions, one would never leave the dock.

Still, the northern horizon steadily looked darker, hazier, and more threatening. Some fifteen years earlier I'd been caught in almost the same spot. My wife and I had been cruising the lower Potomac in a twenty-four-foot Dolphin, a keel-centerboard sloop designed by Sparkman and Stephens. We were crossing from the Yeocomico River, in Virginia, to Herring Creek, on the Maryland side, a distance of less than ten miles. A thunderstorm threatened, but we were confident that we could secure a safe anchorage before the storm hit. Only two miles from our destination, however, Evelyn noticed a small motorboat evidently in distress a mile off Piney Point. We could see a person frantically waving, and we turned back to help. It was tough, slow going to windward, but we made steady progress. Then, when we were only a few hundred yards away, the boat suddenly raced off. Evidently the skipper or his crew had managed to get the engine started, and they were wasting no time and taking no chances in finding shelter. But we had lost nearly half an hour and were more than two miles from *our* safe haven. With the storm bearing down on us, we had only one option: we anchored in the lee of the breakwater behind Piney Point, with marginal protection from wind and waves. We later sat out "the storm of the century" in Boot Key Harbor, Florida, in March 1993, and it was child's play compared to that

Piney Point storm. I have never had a more uncomfortable night on a boat, replacing chafing gear on the anchor rode several times during the night and bouncing out of my bunk. The thunderstorm had only lasted an hour or so, but the fierce winds following the frontal passage had lasted well into the following day.

I passed the mouth of the Saint Marys River, which was disfigured by the buildings and towers of Webster Field, a U.S. naval air station. Warfare and aesthetics don't mix — even in architecture. A small single-engine Cessna was doing touch-and-go landings for the entire hour that I had the airfield in sight.

The last time I had sailed on a river — a month earlier, on the Rappahannock — its width was perhaps a hundred yards. Now I was unable to see land on the other side. In the next one hundred miles there would be only one bridge across this majestic river. I had a long way to go. It was only two in the afternoon, and I was already looking for shelter. And then I ran out of wind. The wind didn't gradually drop off: it stopped abruptly. Often, this is associated with an advancing squall line, but not in this case. An increasing number of threatening cumulonimbus clouds towered upriver.

Through the haze I saw several huge buildings looming ahead. These were the dormitories and classrooms on the sixty-acre campus of the Harry Lundeberg School of Seamanship, which had moved to Piney Point in 1967. The school is the largest training facility for deep-sea merchant seafarers and inland waterways boatmen in the United States. In addition to the large buildings there were other, smaller buildings, and even a huge crane. The school's extensive waterfront facilities included ships, tugs, and myriads of small boats. There would be more protection from high winds further up the creek, but I didn't want to spend the night at anchor surrounded by buildings, or lifeboats, or cranes, and I stuck to my earlier choice, now within rowing distance. I furled sail, stowed the spars, and rowed toward an inviting-looking beach a half mile ahead. When the buildings of the school were hidden by a piney point of land, I headed straight for the beach and ran the boat up on the shore.

On the other side of the narrow isthmus I could see the Saint Marys River, no more than a stone's throw across the low marsh. After a short walk on the beach, during which I kept an anxious eye out for the storm in the distance, I rowed into deeper water a few hundred feet from the beach, closed the hatch covers, zipped the dodger onto the gallows, and draped and buttoned my tent around the framework of spars and PVC pipe. Even if the storm passed by, I would be all set in the morning when the mast had to be down for the passage under the bridge.

The storm came close, and there was plenty of rumbling and much rain, but lightning never came near enough to be worrisome. Late in the afternoon the sky cleared and a cool breeze settled in. But I kept the "back porch" in place, since more showers were forecast for later in the evening. It was now more than ten weeks after the longest day of the year, and sunset would occur around seven-thirty. This called for earlier anchoring, cooking, and cleaning, for I had only a small reading light and an emergency flashlight.

At sunset the breeze became more feeble. A few flies (but no mosquitoes) tried to find their way past my screens. I watched the sun dip beyond Piney Point as I dined on my vegetarian chili with tomatoes, okra, and corn. I had made good nine or ten miles, not too bad considering my late launch earlier in the day. If my splendid anchorage was any indication of what lay ahead, I was in for some treats in the ninety-some miles I had yet to traverse.

Among the rivers of the North Atlantic slope the Potomac is second in size only to the Susquehanna, and it has the fourth largest watershed on the East Coast: it drains fourteen thousand square miles in four states and the District of Columbia. The river begins high in the Allegheny Mountains of West Virginia, where the so-called Fairfax Stone marks "the first fountain of Potowmack"; it then sweeps nearly four hundred miles across the piedmont to the Chesapeake, joined at Harpers Ferry by the Shenandoah, its largest tributary.

Five million gallons of water each minute runs by Washington, D.C., where the river becomes tidal. For centuries the river had been used as a convenient sewer. In the 1960s, CBS called the river "a national disgrace," but in the last several decades the river has been cleaned up to a remarkable extent.

That cleanliness seemed to extend to the air. On my first morning on the Potomac, like my last one on the Rappahannock, I was completely enveloped in dense fog. Sky and water were the same color. There was no wind, no waves, no motion. *Fiddler* might just as well have been sitting on her trailer. The glowing red ball at sunrise gave me my bearings, and some minutes later, when the air warmed up, the outline of Price Cove was revealed again.

After having breakfast and putting the boat in order I motored out of the cove and across the creek toward the bridge, the water still smooth as glass. Fifteen minutes later I was through the bridge and could raise the mast. It seemed a useless move, as there was still no wind.

The nameless bay off Piney Point Beach was like a mine field, booby-trapped with crab pots. My mainsheet, singled up because of the very light air, trailed in the water from time to time, picking up the slimy tentacles of the myriad jellyfish. It was hard to believe that Piney Point had once been a popular summer resort (for years a house on the strand had been a sort of summer White House for President James Monroe), but perhaps years ago there were fewer nettles, or fewer swimmers.

How *Fiddler* could move in this airless environment was a mystery. A true "slick calm," Chesapeake watermen would have called it. Still, move she did, probably at less than a half mile per hour. A gull tried over and over again to pick up a floating, dead fish that was much too heavy for the bird to lift into the air. When I sailed closer, the gull finally gave up the attempt.

The abandoned little lighthouse at Piney Point was dwarfed by the superstructure of the oil tanker I had seen steaming up the river the day before, which was unloading her cargo at the giant Piney Point fuel pier, with two tugs standing by. I sailed close by the large vessel and noticed that at the bow she drew nine feet, while her stern showed twenty-three feet. She still had a lot of oil to unload.

Once around the ship, in clear air, I got a nice, steady, ten-knot southwesterly, and *Fiddler* began making good progress toward Ragged Point on the Virginia side, the first of several turns in the river. My destination, which I hoped to reach by lunchtime, was Saint Clements Island, ten miles upriver.

After John Smith's exploration in the summer of 1608 there had been some commercial activity on the Potomac, mostly by fur traders. It was not until 1634 that a permanent settlement on the Potomac was attempted. Two years earlier, Cecilius Calvert had been able to secure from the king of England a charter for "a certaine Countrey in America (now called Maryland, in honour of our gratious Queene) unto the Lord Baltemore." Unable to make the voyage himself, he sent his twenty-four-year-old younger brother, Leonard Calvert, who, "with the other Gentlemen adventurers, and their servants to the number of neere 200. people, imbarked themselves for the voyage, in the good ship called the *Arke,* of 300. tunne and upward, which was attended by his Lordships Pinnace, called the *Dove,* of about 50. tunne." Many of the colonists were Catholics in search of religious tolerance, separation of church and state, equal justice, and representative government. After a relatively fast 121-day passage from the Isle of Wight (including 37 days spent at anchor waiting for favorable winds) the colonists arrived in the Chesapeake in late February, and by early March they had entered the river, which they called the Saint Gregory. Like the earlier name, San Pedro, the name Saint Gregory didn't stick. Then "They sayled up the River, till they came to Heron Island, which is about 14. leagues, and there came to an Anchor under an Island neere unto it, which they called S. Clements. Where they set up a Crosse."

The expedition's spiritual leader was Father Andrew White, a Jesuit. His *Briefe Relation of the Voyage unto Maryland* devoted only a few thousand words to the Chesapeake Bay and the Potomac River, which he clearly liked: "This baye is the most delightfull water I ever saw, between two sweet landes," he wrote; and "This is the sweetest and greatest river I have seene, so that the Thames is but a little finger to it"; and "the place abounds . . . with pleasure."

The original cross, of course, had gone the way of all wood, but a massive, forty-foot-high concrete cross was erected by the state of Maryland in 1934, to commemorate the first Catholic mass celebrated by English settlers in America, on March 25, 1634. (So much for the separation of church and state.) This was what I thought I saw up ahead when I stood up and scanned the horizon. When the white object I saw appeared to move, it dawned on me that I was seeing the narrow white profile of a sailing yacht beating her way out of Breton Bay. I was still much too far away to see the cross.

An hour later, and five miles further on, the wind died again, and the sky clouded over. I was now close enough to make out the monument, which had been partly hidden behind a stand of trees. Saint Clements Island had been named, at the suggestion of Father White, after the patron saint of sailors, who had been martyred by having an anchor fastened around his neck and thrown into the sea. (The voyagers had left England on November 23, Saint Clement's Day.) The island's name became Blackistone Island after it was bought by a family named Blackistone. In 1962 it was officially renamed Saint Clements. Other saints' names abound on charts of the Potomac, proclaiming the religion of the more powerful of the Maryland colonists. These names include Saint Marys City, Saint Catherine Island, Saint George Creek, Saint Inigoes Creek, and Saint Patrick Creek. In 1634 Calvert had given the names "Saint Michaells Poynt" and "Saint Gregories Poynt" to what we now know as Points Lookout and Smith, at the Potomac's entrance. Smith Creek, just below the Saint Marys River, had been named Trinity Creek until the Protestant Rebellion in 1689. But the chart also showed Protestant Point just inside Breton Bay. About half of the first group of immigrants were Protestants. Cecilius Calvert had instructed his brother Leonard to "Treate the Protestants with as much mildness and favour as Justice will permitt."

The day turned out to be a carbon copy of the day before. The air turned hazy, and the wind went a bit further into the west, forcing me to beat toward the island. Although the wind remained very light, I was still making better time under sail than I would have made rowing. Finally, around one in the afternoon, I arrived for a very late lunch on Saint Clements.

I was the only visitor. There were large piers on the north side of the island to accommodate the tour boats and other vessels that visit regularly in the summer, but they were deserted this late in the season, except for hundreds of gulls occupying all the available pilings. It was not easy to find a clear spot, free of bird droppings, to which to tie up, so that I could climb ashore.

Saint Clements, like Jamestown Island, must have been an inviting place to stop after a long and arduous journey. But it was, as Father White wrote, "not above 400 acres, and therefore too little to seat upon for us." (Today, only one-tenth of that acreage remains.) Calvert then explored the Potomac in the little *Dove* and negotiated with the Indians, and several weeks later the fleet turned downriver again to settle along the banks of the Saint George's River (later called the Saint Marys), where they had "bought the space of thirtie miles of ground . . . , for axes, hoes, cloth and hatchets." Although the colony was named Maryland, when Charles I suggested to Lord Baltimore that the new colony be named after his wife, Queen Henrietta Maria, the new town was named after another Mary. "Saint Maries" became the fourth permanent English settlement in America.

After a picnic ashore, I walked around the island for half an hour, admired the vistas, and kept a weather eye on the sky. The Virginia shore was barely visible, three miles to the south. Nothing was left of the lighthouse that had been built here in 1851 and stood for more than one hundred years, until it burned to the ground in 1956. The island had once been extensively farmed, and there were few trees. Still, it was a pleasant place in which to poke around, especially so since I was its sole explorer.

I should have sailed straight across the river to Nomini Bay or Currioman Bay, both an easy reach, a few miles to the south, and both with plenty of anchorages, especially for shallow-draft boats. (How could I have resisted a creek called Poor Jack, with a depth of one-half foot showing on the chart?) But instead I headed for the high cliffs further up the river, and a little creek seven miles upstream called Popes Creek.

There are two creeks called Popes on the Potomac—one in Virginia, the other in Maryland. I was headed for the one in Virginia. *A Cruising Guide to the Chesapeake* allowed that "Popes Creek is too shallow to enter by boat." The cliffs on the Virginia side, called Nomini, Stratford, and Horsehead, are among the most striking shorelines on the rivers of the Chesapeake, and I skirted past them to search for the tiny opening that would shelter me for the night. The National Weather Service, I had just learned from my weather radio, had issued a "severe thunderstorm watch" that was in effect until ten that evening. I would have to forgo the 13-million-year-old, fossil-laden cliffs and beaches of this shore, and find a snug haven. The wind had picked up, the water became rough, and the ensuing beat to windward was not pleasurable.

Daniel Defoe, in *Moll Flanders,* written in 1722, mentioned the Rappahannock and York Rivers (Moll had a plantation on the York), and had this to say about the stretch of river where I now struggled, and which he never visited:

> In the next place we were full a hundred miles [*sic*] up Potomac River, in a part which they call Westmoreland County, and as that river is by far the greatest in Virginia, and I have heard say it is the greatest river in the world that falls into another river, and not directly into the sea, so we had base weather in it, and were frequently in great danger; for though they call it but a river, 'tis frequently so

broad, that when we were in the middle, we could not see land on either side for many leagues together.

I was in the middle of the river, but I could see land on either side. I just needed to get to it. The skies grew more threatening, and the entrance to Popes Creek proved elusive. After the cliffs, a row of riverfront beach cottages appeared. Then I saw a little indentation in the river's edge, and I followed some crab-pot floats into the narrow inlet. Two small, almost submerged jetties at right angles to the channel confused me, my rudder kicked up, and I lost steering control. There were no more crab pots, and there was no way to know where the deep water was. I felt my way in, using my rudder blade as a depthfinder. Inside the inlet I was confronted by a maze of little islands, and it was impossible to tell which channel to select. I didn't dare go in much further, although I had entered on a rising tide. Had it been a low tide, I would have gone in further, but I had forgotten my tide tables, and the tidal predictions I could hear on my little radio, which were for Hampton Roads, were totally useless on the Potomac.

Still, I was out of harm's way, surrounded by marshes, and although the current was fierce, at two or three knots, I was safe from high winds. In the distance, the only structure in sight was Wakefield, George Washington's birthplace. It was not the original house, which had burned, but a painstakingly reconstructed replica. No doubt the creek had once been considerably deeper, for it was not likely that a Virginia planter would have lived in a place that could not be reached by water.

Once again, the weather forecast was just that: a prediction. The storms, to my relief, never materialized. At eight I could no longer see the beautiful house in the distance, and I slept quietly and soundly until dawn.

In 1906, there appeared in an obscure publication called *The Cruiser* an article by Ross L. Fryer, describing a two-week cruise on the Potomac River on a yacht called the *Janet.*

"If there is any place," he wrote, "which can outpoint the beauties of this river . . . I would go far to see it." The article continued: "It has always seemed strange to me that the Potomac River is not used more by yachtsmen for cruising. The shores, Maryland off to port, and Virginia on the starboard side going down, abound in places of historical interest; the people met are, as a rule, fine specimens of American open-heartedness, and the river itself affords an ample variety of moods to satisfy the most restless and fastidious yachting crank; its calms are the deadest; its storms are the strongest; yet hardly five miles separates the numerous harbors and coves into which a yacht may scud, if it be too much for her, or the heart of her captain fails completely."

I wondered whether I was a "restless and fastidious yachting crank." I had seen a few of the river's calms; I had escaped, so far, its storms; and I had yet to meet any "specimens of American open-heartedness." But I was ready.

After breakfast, a salt-water dip (the current was far too swift for swimming), and a fresh-water shower, I motored out of the creek. Given the fact that the current was flooding, I could not have sailed or rowed out of this haven against the three-knot current unless I had been prepared to wait several hours. But the dawn had been gorgeous, and there was a hint of a breeze outside. The tide was at nearly the same stage it had been at when I had come in the night before, and the rudder touched in several spots, but once I was back out in the river it looked as though I'd be rewarded with a glorious sail. I wanted to get started early to outdistance the cold front that was now definitely going to arrive later in the day, and by 7:30 A.M. I was out on the river. The caveat of the *Cruising Guide to the Chesapeake* notwithstanding, I rated my anchorage a 10. It was beautiful, and had protection and privacy.

The Potomac began to narrow here, and I welcomed it. The enormous width of the river had seemed overwhelming, especially because of the time *Fiddler* and I had spent earlier in the year in the narrow reaches of the upper Rappahannock.

The breeze came hard out of the southwest, the typical preamble to a frontal passage. Off the mouth of Mattox Creek, which was a couple of miles wide with a lot of fetch from the southwest, I reefed my sail. *Fiddler* settled down and behaved beautifully, her sail now reduced to about half its full size, still propelling us at a decent clip. Mattox Creek rates the tiniest of footnotes in American history: In 1657 the *Seahorse of London* arrived here to load tobacco, but sank during a sudden storm. Its second officer was John Washington. He elected to stay in Virginia, married, and founded the family that was to produce the "Father of the Country."

There were now many more homes along the shores of the Potomac than I had seen along any of the other rivers, but I was approaching Colonial Beach, once a favorite bathing resort.

As I was musing on the rapidity of change and the vagaries of architecture, reality entered my tiny world in the form of a high-speed U.S. Navy patrol boat carrying a large red flag.

"Do you know that you're entering a firing range?" its skipper asked. I had seen alarming notations on the chart—"Lower Danger Area," "Middle Danger Area," and "Upper Danger Area"—but I was ignorant of their meaning. "Where are you headed?"

I was loath to reveal my long-range plans. "Washington, D.C.," sounded overly ambitious, and so I allowed that the nearest bridge over the Potomac, some eight miles away, was the object of my nautical dreams.

"Captain," the boat's driver said, with what I thought was a measure of respect considering the size of my craft, "you can go across the river to Cobb Island, and skirt the Maryland shore. Otherwise, you must stay here. We start firing in five minutes. The river will be open again at lunchtime."

Going to Cobb Island would take me ten miles out of my way, an exercise in futility, except perhaps for a motorboat. I had about three hours to wait. So much for my attempt to outpace the expected cold front. A few minutes after nine, a huge explosion a few miles across the river scotched any plans I might have had to evade the patrol boat's edict. An enormous column of water spurted up, and I knew that I was, like it or not, in the confines of the U.S. Naval Weapons Laboratory at Dahlgren, Virginia.

I was allowed to skirt the Virginia shore and sail past Bluff Point, into Rosier Creek. I carefully stayed away from the dashed purple line on the chart which ran from the Range Boat Station through various white and orange buoys and then dead-ended on a point of land called Pumpkin Neck. Except for a few crabbers working close to shore, the area was deserted, and there were some splendid, fifty-foot-high cliffs. While staying on the safe side of what the *Pilot* called "Line of Fire Buoy S," I slid *Fiddler* onto the beach to wait out the show. There was sporadic firing. But it was pleasant in the lee of the cliffs, the water was deep right up to the shore, and a narrow, sandy beach allowed for a short walk.

After my walk, I rowed out a short distance from the cliffs, for the wind had gone light again, and the day was rapidly warming up. The bridge, the only one on the Potomac until the District of Columbia, emerged from the haze along with a couple of smokestacks that belonged to an electric power plant. On the Virginia side there was a weird-looking and ugly collection of buildings that belonged to the Navy's Dahlgren facility. Many of the structures were festooned with antennas, dishes, and other paraphernalia that one would presumably need to test artillery shells or other explosives. Time and again, on all the rivers I sailed during these cruises, military installations hideously disfigured the waterfront with their shameful architecture and undisciplined land use.

Still, if the eye didn't wander toward Dahlgren, or the bridge, it would be hard to find a more pleasant spot to spend a few idle hours. At 11:20 I saw the range patrol boats speeding back toward the Dahlgren pier on Upper Machodoc Creek. I took this as a sign that the exercise was over, and lunch was being served. The whole thing had been like a twenty-one-gun salute that lasted two hours.

I shook out the reef, made sail in the diminishing breeze, and released the crab-pot float to which I'd been tethered for the last hour.

Then a thought occurred to me: suppose those navy guys had gone in for a short break but would come roaring back before I'd gotten out of the restricted area? The bosun's mate had said that he'd let me know when I could proceed again, but the patrol boat had not let me know. Perhaps they'd tried to call me on the radio! I started the engine, and thirty minutes later I was clear of the range and under the bridge. This was the narrowest part of the river so far, but it was still more than a mile and a half wide.

Next to the bridge on the Maryland side was a small marina on a small dredged basin that could be reached through a narrow, jettied inlet. I needed to take on fuel, and forage for some other supplies. I squeezed a gallon of gas into my fuel tank: $1.49. As I made my way further north, the price of fuel was increasing. When I walked past the pump to pay my bill, I noticed that the other side of the pump read 1.5 gallons. Two Maryland marine policemen were eating lunch on a bench outside, with their backs to the water and to their boat, and one of them had noticed my confusion.

"The lower number is what you got. The price's the same whatever it says," he assured me. No hanky-panky here, I thought, with the law keeping track of my purchases. At least I knew how much oil to add.

At the marina store I bought some nuts and a six-pack of beer.

"Don't you want it cold?" the clerk demanded. I explained about my lack not only of refrigeration but of an ice chest. He talked me into buying the cold beer anyway. "At least the first one will be cold," he insisted. Still, a fellow who only bought one gallon of gas and didn't want his beer cold was probably not exactly his average customer. I tried some small talk.

"What's the name of the bridge?" I asked, staring overhead through the window. The chart had merely said "Potomac River Bridge."

"Very nice," I heard.

"It's beautiful," I agreed. "Very nice indeed."

"Harry Nice," he repeated over the loud country music on his radio. "Harry Nice. He was a politician or something."

"From Maryland or from Virginia?" I asked.

"Oh, Maryland, for sure. We own the Potomac, you know."

I knew I was back in Maryland.

I rapidly left the Harry W. Nice Bridge behind me as I reached north, on an ever-building warm southwesterly and a favoring current. The current at the narrowing of the river in the ten-mile stretch between Persimmon and Maryland Points is the strongest on the river, sometimes exceeding three knots, and it affected the attempted escape of John Wilkes Booth after he assassinated President Lincoln.

Near Maryland's Popes Creek, which enters the Potomac a mile or two above Persimmon Point, was kept the small fishing skiff that allowed Booth to cross to Virginia. He had arranged to have a small boat waiting for him at Port Tobacco, five miles further north, but he broke his leg during the escape from Ford's Theater and had to seek medical help before proceeding. With his co-conspirator, Davey Herold, he sought out the hapless Dr. Samuel Mudd (who was later wrongfully imprisoned for his ministrations). The following day Booth and Herold tried slowly to make their way to Port Tobacco and the waiting boat, but they had to avoid the roads through the countryside, and managed to get lost in Zekiah Swamp, a marshy wilderness a few miles from the Potomac. They ended up being helped and hidden by two Confederate sympathizers, Samuel Cox and Thomas Jones. Jones promised "to bring [Booth] food every day, and to get him across the river, if possible, just as soon as it would not be suicidal to make the attempt." One week after the assassination, after nightfall, Booth, Herold, and Jones made their way toward Popes Creek, three or four miles away, where Jones kept a small fishing boat. The trio made the first part of the trip on horseback and then proceeded on foot. Jones described the subsequent events in his *J. Wilkes Booth,* published in 1893:

> The path was steep and narrow and for three men to walk down it abreast, one of them being a cripple, to whom every step was torture, was not the least difficult part of that night's work.

But the Potomac, that longed-for goal, at last was near.

It was nearly calm now, but the wind had been blowing during the day and there was a swell upon the river, and as we approached, we could hear its sullen roar. It was a mournful sound coming through the darkness. . . .

At length we reached the shore and found the boat. . . . It was a flat bottomed boat about twelve feet long, of a dark lead color. . . .

We placed Booth in the stern with an oar to steer; Herold took the bow-seat to row. Then lighting a candle which I had brought for the purpose—I had no lantern—and carefully shading it with an oilcloth coat belonging to one of the men, I pointed out on the compass Booth had with him the course to steer. "Keep to that," I said, "and it will bring you into Machodoc Creek. Mrs. Quesenberry lives near the mouth of this creek. If you tell her you come from me I think she will take care of you.". . .

I pushed the boat off and it glided out of sight into the darkness.

I stood on the shore and listened till the sound of the oars died away in the distance.

Upper Machodoc Creek was where I had spent the morning waiting for the range to open; it was five or six miles downriver. Mathias Point, directly across from Popes Creek, is only a little more than two miles distant. The Potomac here makes an abrupt, one-hundred-degree turn. In the haste of the moment, Jones failed or forgot to warn Herold and Booth of the flooding current. The little boat, unable to stem the tide, was carried upriver along the Maryland shore and ended up nearly six miles *upstream* in a small tributary of Nanjemoy Creek. There Booth and Herold remained in concealment until dark the following evening, when they made another attempt, on the ebb tide. They landed on the Virginia shore, in tiny Gambo Creek, a mile above Upper Machodoc Creek, after a journey of nearly a dozen miles. With help, they made their way to the Rappahannock, which they crossed, still undetected, at Port Royal. They found refuge on the Garrett Farm, where they posed as

Confederate veterans. Union cavalrymen found them a few days later. In the ensuing drama Herold surrendered, but Booth was fatally wounded by a shot fired by one of the soldiers, and died at daybreak. In the last century, Popes Creek has completely shoaled up.

With the weather bureau forecasting winds of fifteen to twenty-five knots, with higher gusts, I needed to find a *very* protected anchorage for the night to come. Following the Potomac's course further was out of the question. There would be no decent anchorages for fifteen miles, even for a shoal-draft vessel such as *Fiddler*. I had about six hours of daylight left, but perhaps only a few hours until the frontal passage and the ensuing gale.

I noticed on the chart that Goose Creek, the first and only indentation in the otherwise straight shores of the short Port Tobacco River, would be sheltered from the west and northwest: it would be my home for the night. I covered the six miles to my destination in less than an hour, and my attention never wavered from keeping the boat sailing—and upright.

When I reached the mouth of the Port Tobacco River, I welcomed the protection the river offered. It had been a thrilling sail, but I should have reefed several miles back. The river's shores were low on the western side but very high on the eastern side. The Indian name for the tributary was Pertafacco, meaning "in the hollow of the hills." John Smith explored here, and on his map showed an Indian village called Potapaco. Although a tobacco port for a short time in the seventeenth century, the Port Tobacco River had silted up so badly by 1700 that ocean-going ships could no longer reach the port.

Goose Creek had a small marina and campground near its entrance. I sailed past the boats and trailers until I reached the marsh at the creek's westernmost edge, and then anchored in about three feet of water at the very shallow head of the creek. The marina held about a dozen small cruising sailboats and several dozen small motorboats. It was probably a handy location for both kinds of skippers, since it allowed good fishing for the motorboat crowd, and easy access to the wide waters of the Potomac for the sailors.

Despite my proximity to the marshes, I wasn't worried about insects. If it was going to blow as hard as was forecast, mosquitoes would be the least of my problems. Nevertheless, I put up my tent after lowering the mast. I was no sooner zipped in than it started to rain a little. The rain stopped after five minutes, but it looked as if there would be a lot more to come. Heavy, dark clouds glowered from the north. It was only midafternoon, early for me to stop, but I was glad that I was securely anchored, and took advantage of the quiet to take a long nap.

A different motion awakened me an hour later. The rain had started again, and the wind had picked up. *Fiddler* was presenting me with rapidly changing views of my anchorage—now showing a verdant, pristine marsh, now giving me a glimpse of the marina in the distance, and then swerving past the campground back to the marsh again. Philip Bolger, *Fiddler*'s designer, had written that one of the Dovekie's failings was that "she sails around her anchor in an infuriating way." I had, of course, noticed that tendency often—but never, I thought, had I seen it demonstrated in such an aggressive way. The radio reported that gusts with speeds of up to twenty-seven miles per hour had been reported at Washington National Airport. I didn't think we'd seen more than twenty knots, or if we had, our protection was so excellent that it seemed far less than that.

Shortly the rain stopped and the skies began to clear. The wind settled into the northwest at a steady fifteen knots, considerably less than what I had been expecting. Still, I was grateful for the haven and the peaceful night it promised.

Dinner, just before sunset, consisted of rice and beans (or, more accurately, rice with beans, since I had cooked far too much rice for one person), a sinful Pepperidge Farm cookie called Chesapeake, and a cockpit-temperature beer. All looked well with the world, and once the sunset's glow had gone, and pitch dark had descended on Goose Creek, I went to sleep. If I dragged anchor I would end up in the marsh, not the marina.

There was a breeze at dawn, but the wind was rather calmer than it had been when I went to sleep. Like the severe thunderstorm watch of the previous night, the twenty-five-knot business seemed to have been a localized affair. But it was cold—in the upper fifties, a temperature I had not felt in many months. I rummaged through my duffel bag to find a pair of long pants and a sweater.

I had a long day ahead of me, and most of it would be battling headwinds. But I wanted, needed, to take advantage of the breeze, for in the next few days, as the high-pressure center moved closer to the Potomac area, there would be little or no wind. I fortified myself with a hot breakfast: poached eggs, corned beef, and toast, along with orange juice and coffee. A little after seven the sun rose above the trees along the shore, and I dismantled the tent and got *Fiddler* ready for her day's voyage.

I was tempted to run with the wind up the Port Tobacco River, to skirt the river's high cliffs, which in places were 170 feet high, and to explore to the head of navigation. But as I sailed out of Goose Creek and around Windmill Point, the broad Potomac looked comfortable enough, with the wind not quite straight down the river at around ten miles per hour. I settled down to a pleasant sail on a starboard tack. Then, as Yogi Berra is reputed to have said, "it was déjà vu all over again." A boat flying a red flag was running toward me at high speed, much as the range patrol boat had done the day before. But it turned out to be a crabber with an enormous Confederate flag flying from his antenna, headed back to port.

I was beginning to suspect that the weather forecaster was suffering from dyslexia and had reversed things. The gale we were supposed to have had last night was starting to develop in the very stretch of the Potomac in which I was sailing. I had only been on the river for a few miles—for half an hour—when it began to blow, the breeze quickly rising to more than fifteen knots, occasionally gusting to more than twenty. I had the current with me, but as it opposed the wind, the waves grew disproportionately larger. Off the mouth of Nanjemoy Creek I reefed, reducing my sail area by nearly one-half, and a semblance of comfort returned. They say, "Reef early," and by 7:30 I had done just that.

Reefing is a simple procedure with Dovekies, merely a matter of partially lowering the sail, hooking rings on the luff and leach (the two angled sides of the triangular sail) to hooks on the sprit and the base of the mast, hoisting the sail taut again, tightening the (inelegantly named) snotter, and then tying the five knots in the reefpoints which hold the rolled-up foot (bottom) of the sail. It takes longer to describe it than to do it. I seldom regretted that I had reefed, for it usually made the motion more comfortable and the sailing safer. And if conditions changed for the better, it took only moments to reverse the procedure.

When the crabbing boat disappeared behind Mathias Point, *Fiddler* was the only vessel on this stretch of the river. It had been very different a century earlier. The keeper of the light at Maryland Point noted in his log that during daylight hours on August 16, 1898, 184 sailing vessels and 31 steamers had passed the lighthouse. The lighthouse keeper seems not to have considered it an unusual day.

I hugged the windward shore, barely able to lay Maryland Point, seven or eight miles distant. The river was covered with whitecaps. Short, steep waves, three feet high, occasionally breaking, and throwing spray around the boat, thwarted any rapid progress. What had started as a relaxed sail was rapidly becoming a wet, bouncy nightmare that required all my attention. Every once in a while a rogue wave, higher than and out of synch with the others, would stop *Fiddler* dead in her tracks. Although I was still able to sail and keep moving, no matter how slowly, I knew that once I rounded Maryland Point, where the Potomac radically changes direction again, I would have to begin tacking to make any gain to windward. It was a dismaying prospect. The object of my aspiration became Potomac Creek, a small tributary four miles beyond Maryland

Point, and the first available shelter if I didn't want to run back into Nanjemoy Creek.

And so, rather than relinquishing my hard-won ten or twelve miles, I plowed on, and after what seemed like an endless time I gained the relative peace of Potomac Creek and then the total peace of Accokeek Creek, a smaller tributary. It had been the longest and most demanding sail to windward that I recalled having made in *Fiddler*. I vowed to take the aphorism "Gentlemen don't sail to windward" more seriously in the future. But the creek was serene, and the shrimp salad I had for lunch was scrumptious. After lunch I took a short nap to rest up from the rigors of the morning.

After a two-hour interlude at anchor I ventured forth again. The winds appeared to have abated somewhat and were now gusting less often and with a lesser intensity. The Potomac was still rambunctious, but there was nowhere near the chaotic scene the river had presented earlier in the day. After a few hundred yards in the open river I decided to shake the reef out. (I've never figured out where the "shake" comes from. Certainly there is no shaking involved!)

I was now headed for a place called Youbedam, the southern point at the entrance to Aquia Creek, the next upriver shelter. But I'll be damned if the wind didn't back into the west a little so that I was able to easily steer for Sandy Point, at Mallows Bay, eight miles up the river. Sailing was still very challenging, but pleasantly so, and I made steady progress. I skirted Mallows Bay, a shallow indentation on the Maryland side of the river which was littered with the burned hulks of dozens of ships, the Ghost Fleet of Mallows Bay.

When the United States entered the Great War in the spring of 1917, the Allied vessels that were lost to German U-boats numbered several hundred every month. Wrote the historian Donald G. Shomette, "Under the auspices of the newly-formed United States Shipping Board, a bold scheme was launched to build and field a massive armada of wooden freight steamers for Atlantic duty. Such a fleet, it was pre-

dicted, could be constructed cheaply, would not tie up the great ship-
yards already involved in steel ship construction, and could be produced
with semi-skilled manpower. The vessels, so easily and rapidly produced,
were virtually expendable."

Expendable they were, but nobody could have imagined how expendable. It was hoped that a thousand ships could be built in eighteen
months, but those months saw only a nightmare of bureaucratic inepti-
tude and colossal, proliferating, paperwork. The first steamship was not
ready for sea until more than a year later—and was deemed unsea-
worthy by the U.S. Navy. When the war ended, in November 1918, only
134 vessels had been completed (out of 731 contracted for), and none had
made it across the Atlantic Ocean.

As Shomette explained: "Despite Congressional indignation, the
ships continued to slide off the ways for delivery. By mid-1919, 174 had
been put into service, even as the government sought to sell off the
fleet piecemeal. On September 27, 1920, the Shipping Board moved to
dispose of the largest component of the grandest white elephant produced to that date by a nation at war—285 leaking wooden ships totaling
994,235 deadweight tons. The principal bulk of the fleet, including 21
ships built in the Middle Atlantic District, lay at anchor in the James
River at Claremont. They were being kept pumped out and afloat by
two tugs and a small army of men at a cost of $50,000 per month. The
ramshackle armada was offered for sale as a single unit 'as is and where
is.' Each vessel had cost the nation between $700,000 and $1,000,000, or
about $170 per deadweight ton."

Two years later, 212 of these ships were sold for scrap for $750,000.
In the fall of 1925 the first flotilla of hulls was towed into Mallows Bay,
and torched. Eventually 169 ships were burned on the river. In the next
decade, salvors continued to strip the derelicts of metal, bootleggers
operated stills, and in the floating community that sprang up around the
little bay, five floating brothels are said to have been in operation, affec-
tionately and collectively known as "Potomac River Arks." Hardly any

evidence remains above the water, but the outlines of many of the ships can still be seen in the shallows of Mallows Bay.

As the afternoon wore on and the seas and wind continued to subside, a few boats were venturing out to enjoy this brilliant Saturday afternoon, and by late afternoon, as I sailed past the Quantico Marine Base, I had counted three sailboats and seven or eight motorboats—more than I had seen in all my previous days on the river put together. I stayed close to the Maryland shore, which was far prettier, with high, wooded cliffs, than the ugly military-industrial facility two miles across the river.

At six o'clock, at the mouth of Chicamuxen Creek, the wind died. I had planned to anchor in this creek because, judging from the chart, it offered good protection from wind and waves. I struck my sail and began motoring into the anchorage. As soon as I left the wide Potomac and entered the creek, however, I saw that it was densely covered with hydrilla, aquatic plants that were first introduced in the American southeast and have found their way to some rivers on the Chesapeake. The plants have turned out to be difficult to eradicate. My engine sputtered and quit in protest: the spinach-like leaves had choked off the water supply to the jet pump. I needed to swim under the boat and clear the six-inch intake screen, and I didn't look forward to a swim on this very cool day. But the water was warm, and I didn't have to anchor, for the mass of leaves kept *Fiddler* from drifting away on the nearly windless waters. And the jellyfish had been left behind many miles ago. Once the intake screen was cleared I rowed the boat back into clear water and motored back out into the Potomac. Chicamuxen was not going to be my anchorage for the night. I had another two miles to go to Mattawoman Creek, the next protected anchorage, a winding waterway, which I reached just before twilight. I anchored in a cove just beyond the entrance, exhausted, after one of the longest and most demanding days of my cruises. A few minutes later, my floating home was rocked and rolled into disarray by the reverberating wakes of several passing motorboats darting up the channel. I moved a half mile further up the creek and anchored close to shore, far away from the channel. I had just enough energy left to heat a can of mushroom soup before crawling into my sleeping bag.

I was probably still in the REM portion of my sleep cycle when the rock and roll began again. If ever you want to sleep late, don't anchor in a protected cove on Mattawoman Creek on a Sunday morning in September. Bass fishing is big business, and the first bassboats roared out of the creek before there was a glimmer of a hope of dawn. I peeked out through one of my oar-ports and thought I was looking at a rush-hour traffic jam on shore. In the nearly pitch-black darkness I saw the lights of dozens of bassboats, green and white showing, heading out slowly toward the mouth of the creek. (The no-wake restrictions in the channel are rigidly enforced by the Maryland Natural Resources Police.) It looked a little like cars crawling along a riverside drive.

The crews of several boats that weren't participating in the outbound procession had started casting near my anchorage, and it had been one of these, approaching slowly yet throwing a big wake, that had awakened me. The rolling propelled me out of the sack into a record low temperature, according to the cheery voice of the National Oceanographic and Atmospheric Administration on my weather radio. Fall would not be long in arriving. As the sky lightened, wisps of fog rose from the water, making for an eerie seascape and occasionally obscuring my bass-fishing neighbors.

Hunting and fishing were prohibited on Sundays during most of the seventeenth century. Members of "His Lordship's Assembly" in Maryland viewed with alarm "the wicked and profane licentiousness of severall persons inhabiting or travelling into this Province to Spend Sunday in the bodily Excercise or occupation of fishing." The assembly later ordered that no one be allowed to fish on future Sundays "with any Netts, Tramells, Saines, Hookes or Lines." The fine for infringement was one hundred pounds of tobacco. The reward for catching the biggest fish on this Sunday could be in the tens of thousands of dollars.

A Dovekie in the best of circumstances is not a very private abode. Still, the fishermen, intent on their quest, completely ignored my morning rituals as I brushed my teeth, fixed my breakfast, and dismantled my tent, trying to speed up the drying of the canvas after the heavy morning dew. Over several cups of coffee I had plenty of opportunity to observe a number of bass fishermen, and managed to come to these totally unscientific conclusions about how to qualify as a bass fisherman:

— You must be male.
— You must have a partner, also male.
— You and your partner must dress identically.
— You must wear a baseball cap, which must be worn backward when the boat is moving.
— You must have a boat with swivel chairs, and it must be painted in a flecked metallic finish.
— You must have two engines: one that can go one hundred miles per hour, and another that can go one mile per hour.
— You must not talk to anyone, including your partner.

The fishermen were not having any luck, but they weren't going away, either. A breeze came up out of the south, warming and dispersing the fog. I decided that I could find more privacy on the river than I could in the creek. I rowed to the Sweden Point Marina nearby, where I replenished my water supply and discovered that on the weekend I had chosen to visit Mattawoman Creek, the creek was the site of one of the biggest, most lucrative professional bass-fishing tournaments in the country. I found out that one of those paint-flecked bassboats could easily cost forty thousand dollars, and that it was possible to win that much in a day of fishing. I also saw a *trailer* on the parking lot which was decorated in flecked metallic paint.

The bassboats out on the river looked like waterbugs from a distance, and sounded like angry bees when they passed close by. But a mile or so outside Mattawoman Creek the hectic activity subsided, and I could settle down to enjoy a spanking breeze. The morning warmed up as quickly as the evening had cooled off the night before. I was sailing the last wide part of the Potomac, past Occoquan and Belmont Bays. Soon the river would narrow to less than a mile opposite Mount Vernon, and then to less than half a mile at Fort Washington. Perhaps because the river was narrower, and both shores were high, wooded, and undeveloped, I felt that this stretch of the Potomac could vie with parts of the James and the Rappahannock for the "most beautiful" award.

The wonderful wind and weather helped fuel that feeling as *Fiddler* screamed upriver. In late morning a few small sailboats and windsurfers appeared. I enjoyed an informal race with a twenty-two-foot keelboat with four people aboard, a race *Fiddler* won hand over fist, but whose results became less satisfactory when I realized that my competitor was teaching his crew to sail and showing them different sail maneuvers.

It was gratifying to see that this historic stretch of the river had remained quite undeveloped. This would have surprised George Washington, for he wrote in 1796,

> The rise in the value of landed property, in this country, has been progressive, ever since my attention has been turned to the subject (now more than 40 years); but for the last three or four of that period, it has increased beyond all calculation. . . . I do not hesitate to pronounce that, the Lands on the Waters of Potomack will, in a few years, be in greater demand, and in higher estimation than in any other part of the United States.

Late in the morning I stopped at Mount Vernon, which has a substantial pier and a buoyed channel. The historic site receives a million visitors a year, but few come by boat. This day, however, a large tour boat was tied to the pier and made for an excellent, protected lee. As I sailed to the pier I saw hundreds of Japanese tourists reembarking after touring George Washington's home. Washington had inherited the house that his father had built, and enlarged and expanded it. He also increased the size of the estate to eight thousand acres, of which today only five hundred acres remain.

After the tour boat left I was totally unprotected from wind and waves, and I did not dare leave my boat so vulnerable. I set sail again, regretting that I had no bell aboard, for sailors are supposed to ring their fogbells as they sail past Mount Vernon, a custom that is said to have been started on Washington's death.

Twenty minutes later and two miles upriver, I ran into wide but shallow Piscataway Creek for lunch. It was only noon, and I had covered more than fifteen miles already, a splendid, satisfying Sunday morning sail. Piscataway Creek has a marina, and there are several houses on its northern shore, but the creek is otherwise not developed. It is very wide, and its southern shore is a protected habitat, with magnificent views of the Potomac and Fort Washington, whose site George Washington personally selected: he could see the headland from his porch.

Once at anchor in the bight behind Mockley Point, I decided to stay put. I was in shouting distance of Alexandria (in fact, I had seen the Woodrow Wilson Bridge, part of the Capital Beltway, six miles to the north as I turned into Piscataway Creek), and I was pretty sure that beauty and privacy on the river would be in short supply as I sailed into the District of Columbia. And the long and strenuous sail of the day before, and the exhilarating romp this morning, were beginning to take their toll. After lunch I had a long nap, and then took a midafternoon swim in the clear (and now completely fresh) water. A small canoe was the only watercraft that came close to my anchorage. The boats going to and from the marina all used the marked channel a half mile across the creek. In late afternoon I rowed to the marina to make a phone call and arrange for my retrieval from the river. This night would, presumably, be my last night on the river. I was within a dozen miles of the head of navigation, which would be easily reached in one day.

Once back and anchored again in my serene anchorage, I rummaged through my supplies for the makings of a last dinner on the

Potomac. I found some canned salmon and baby shrimps and managed to concoct a decent meal. It occurred to me that it was weird that someone who liked seafood as much as I do was not a fisherman. I might have had fresh blue crabs, or even large-mouth bass.

I watched the creek, and then the river, become smooth as a satin sheet as the wind subsided and the distant boat wakes slowly dissipated. The sunset was as spectacular as the sunrise had been. I left the mast up and didn't bother with my tent, hoping that it wouldn't be cold, wouldn't be buggy, and wouldn't rain. It didn't rain. It was only a little buggy. Robert Beverley had written a few hundred years earlier that "Musketaes are . . . troublesome," but that he had an "easie Remedy. Let him but set open his Windows at Sun-set, and shut them again before the Twilight be quite shut in, and all the Musketaes in the Room, will go out at the Windows, and leave the Room clear." I fell asleep trying to decipher the true meaning of the sentence.

I was up before sunrise, and I dressed while still in my sleeping bag. I lit my stove not so much to boil water as to make a pitiful attempt to warm the air in the cockpit. The temperature was not the only repetition of the morning before. What I at first thought was a lot of little boats running along the edge of the river in Virginia turned out to be a steady stream of cars on the parkway, commuters heading for the District, their headlights flashing between stands of trees like horizontal meteor showers.

Even this early, the telltales on the shrouds had begun to stir, promising a decent breeze. But first I had to coax the sun from behind the trees into the open. The stove wasn't doing much to keep me warm. Before seven I had joined the commuters on the way to Washington, D.C., and sometimes I didn't seem to be going much more slowly than they were. The Monday morning rush hour was on.

"When you get eleven fathoms and an ooze on the lead, you are a day's journey from Alexandria," Herodotus had written twenty-five hundred years ago about another Alexandria, five thousand miles to the east.

Although I didn't have a leadline, the chart, off Fort Washington, uncannily showed sixty-six feet—eleven fathoms. And Alexandria, Virginia, was only an hour's journey away—due north on the ever-narrowing Potomac.

A skein of geese, seven in all, flew directly downriver, heading south. Not a minute later, a flight of seven—*seven!*—helicopters flew overhead, also in a V-formation, but headed north toward the nation's capital. Later I found out that the peace accords between Israel and the Palestine Liberation Organization had been signed at the White House on that Monday. No doubt the helicopters were involved in this security-minded event.

At precisely 7 A.M., the first jet had screamed off the seven-thousand-foot main runway of Washington National Airport, on the other side of the Woodrow Wilson Bridge. Fortunately, the airport is closed to jetliners from 9 P.M. to 7 A.M. daily. For the next several hours I was (sometimes painfully) aware of the constant takeoffs and landings of the aircraft, three miles apart, landing lights on for greater visibility even after daylight arrived, the departing flights following the river's course downstream and climbing to their assigned altitudes. It was a mad, awesome, frenzied, and noisy display, regular as clockwork.

Probably celebrating the fact that the weekend was over and the fishermen would leave the river in peace for a few days, fish were jumping all around the boat. What I took to be a very tall smokestack turned out to be, as I got a little closer, the Washington Monument.

With the breeze behind me but the current against me, I was making only about three or four miles per hour. Still, I was going faster than any of the cars stalled in the traffic jam on the bridge. Because of the bridge's fifty-foot clearance, *Fiddler* could easily scoot under it, no doubt to the great relief of the motorists, most of whom probably didn't know that the bridge has a severely restricted opening schedule for non-commercial vessels. As I passed under the bridge, the sun appeared from behind the cloud-bank that had been hiding it since dawn. This now appeared to be the perfect way to enter Washington, D.C.: silently, in a small sailboat, with the warming wind behind, and without traffic snarls or noise abatement procedures.

Alexandria and its redeveloped waterfront are mostly pleasant to look at (although there are some outrageously kitschy townhouse reproductions), but it did not seem like a place for sailors. There was a marina, but it did not look inviting and didn't appear to offer much protection from wakes or waves. Alexandria is where much of Washington eats out, and it is said that there are more than one hundred restaurants squeezed into the tiny, three-hundred-year-old historic district. A large freighter docks occasionally, delivering, of all things, newsprint. A few times a year, one of the large cruise ships calls at the waterfront and whisks people to warmer climes.

Within a dozen miles of metropolitan Washington, there are a score of military installations that together occupy more than fifty miles of Potomac River shoreline. There were several such grim-looking installations on the shore opposite Alexandria: the U.S. Naval Research Laboratory and Bolling Air Force Base.

Despite the horrible noise, I enjoyed the airshow as I sailed past Washington National Airport. When I was flying small planes years ago, noise was the only aspect of aviation that I abhorred. Perhaps that dislike of noise was why sailing, and its silence, had always so appealed to me. Now Boeing 727s and 737s, DC-9s, Fokkers, helicopters, and business jets made for a disagreeable cacophony but a constantly interesting and changing skyscape. Sometimes six or seven aircraft would be in sight all at once. I did not envy the air traffic controllers' jobs. Pilots are not fond of the airport either, euphemistically calling it "challenging."

Although the river was still quite wide here—nearly one mile in width—it was also quite shallow. Dredging had been going on here for nearly two centuries; the airport was itself built on dredged channel sediment. Where the Anacostia River joins the Potomac, there are several marinas and yacht clubs on Washington Channel behind East Potomac Park (also made of dredged sediment).

As I approached the first of the six fixed bridges spanning the Potomac within the District, I reluctantly furled my sail and lowered the mast, then motored slowly up the river, past the Jefferson Memorial and the Tidal Basin (closed off from the river by a huge floodgate), until I reached the bridge that crosses the river from the Lincoln Memorial to Arlington Cemetery, where I could raise the mast and sail again, since that bridge as well as the two subsequent bridges had at least a thirty-foot clearance. The wind remained favorable, and I sailed past the Georgetown waterfront, where the Watergate Apartments and the Kennedy Center occupied much of the real estate.

After the Key Bridge, the river, now less than a quarter of a mile wide, was dotted with large rocks visible just above the surface, and the shores became higher and forested; buildings had disappeared. Captain Smith had written, "Here we found mighty Rocks, growing in some places above the ground as high as the shrubby trees." I sailed past the boulders called the Three Sisters, said to have been named for Indian princesses.

A small skiff was anchored near the shore, its occupant proudly displaying what looked like a ten-pound catfish as I sailed by. Except for the whine and drone of the aircraft flying their approaches, following the river toward the airport, there was no indication of the bustling metropolis surrounding this Eden. Tobias Lear, who for years was George Washington's private secretary, wrote in 1793 that this part of the country was "not exceeded, in fertility of soil and salubrity of air, by any in America, if any in the world; and no part of America can boast of being more healthy than the Potomack in general."

Eventually the high cliffs completely blocked the wind, and I began motoring toward the last bridge over the tidal Potomac, Chain Bridge. This was the site of the first bridge built across the river, a covered wooden bridge built in 1797 and called the Little Falls Bridge. It was a toll bridge; the charge was three cents for a pedestrian, eight cents for a man and a horse. A severe flood in 1804 washed the bridge away, but a few years later a suspension bridge, using chains with iron links, was constructed. It was destroyed by floods in 1810. Although the present structure, built in 1936 of steel and concrete, is the sixth bridge on the site, the name Chain Bridge has stuck.

Near the bridge I had to increase power, and once under the bridge I had to use full power to stem the current. A hundred yards ahead was the white water of a small cataract: the head of navigation. I was 104 miles from the Chesapeake Bay, and I could go no further. The swift current helped make turning around easy in the narrow stream when I reduced power. I floated downstream for a few hundred yards until I found an inviting place to run *Fiddler* onto: a sandy shoal between several huge rocks. I would lunch ashore in the District of Columbia. I tied *Fiddler* to a tree, climbed up on a rock, looked across the narrow stream toward the Virginia side, and ate my lunch in what was surely the most private spot in the District of Columbia.

The nearest ramp was four miles back down the river. After lunch I motored to the Key Bridge, where I found a fresh breeze and some room to sail. After an hour of battling the increasingly gusty southerlies, I turned *Fiddler* back into a motorboat. There was more wind now than I wanted to row against, and it was time for me to head toward the ramp at a small motorboat marina a mile beyond the Arlington Memorial Bridge. It was two o'clock. I had arranged to be hauled out at three, on a rising tide, and the voyage would have to come to an end.

Ramp is the Dutch word for "catastrophe." Although I have been speaking and reading English for decades, the word still holds terror for me. The ramp at the Pentagon Lagoon (so named for its proximity to the famous five-sided building) looked like a catastrophe too. A boat would be floated onto a rickety sort of railway carriage on which the trailer would be secured, and the boat and trailer would then be hauled up a steep incline until the automobile could be reattached to the trailer. I had never seen a contraption like it before, and it did not inspire confidence.

A sign said, "$12 Roundtrip — $7 One Way." This was more money than I had ever paid anywhere else for a ramp fee. What did I expect, though, one thousand feet from the Pentagon? Cost *underruns*?

I had a hard time even paying my seven bucks, however.

"We don't haul sailboats," the lady in the office snarled, not fooled for one minute by the lowered spars.

"It is not a sailboat," I said. That was not a lie. *Fiddler* was registered in the Commonwealth of Virginia as a motorboat. If she hadn't had that little engine I could have registered her as a rowboat—and could have escaped paying certain taxes.

"You sure you don't have a keel under that thing?" she asked suspiciously.

I assured her that *Fiddler*'s bottom had no hidden protuberances. I used words like "no deadrise," and "no rocker."

"When she goes aground she sits upright, like a church," I continued. She liked that metaphor.

"Well, all right," she agreed, and reached for the money.

An hour later, *Fiddler* was crossing the Potomac River on the Capital Beltway at sixty miles per hour. I had hoped that the bridge would be open so that I could stare at the river a little longer.

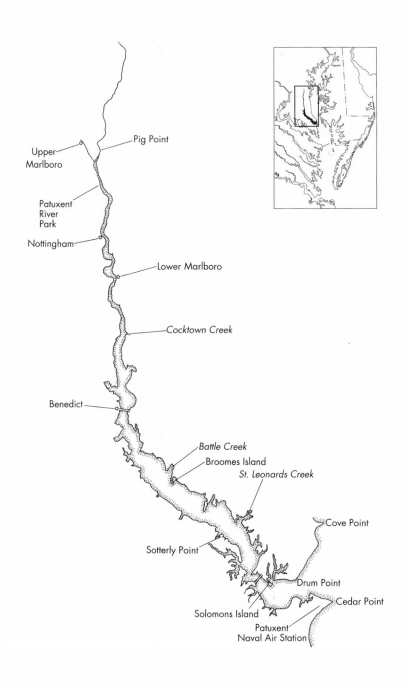

Pig Point

Upper
Marlboro

Patuxent
River
Park

Nottingham

Lower Marlboro

Cocktown Creek

Benedict

Battle Creek

Broomes Island

St. Leonards Creek

Cove Point

Sotterly Point

Drum Point

Cedar Point

Solomons Island

Patuxent
Naval Air Station

The Patuxent

On a sunny, cool morning in early October, I set out from a launching ramp under a bridge near the mouth of the Patuxent River, at Solomons Island. The temperature hovered around fifty degrees, and the
wind was out of the west at ten miles per hour. I had planned to launch
Fiddler in the harbor of Solomons Island, and had made arrangements by
telephone the previous week to slide the boat into the water at a small
marina. "Come anytime. We're open seven days a week," I had heard
on the telephone. When I arrived at the marina's ramp I saw a sign,
suspended from a chain, that read, "Open Seven Days a Week." "Except Tuesdays," an addendum noted in smaller letters. It was Tuesday. I
headed for the public ramp a mile or so upriver.

It took about ten minutes to get the Dovekie ready for sailing: to
stow my clothes and groceries, raise the mast, and bend on the sail.
Then I decided to sail back toward the harbor of Solomons, the largest
settlement on the Patuxent, and take in the whole river from the mouth.

The Patuxent has its source on the eastern slope of Parr's Ridge, in
central Maryland, not far from Frederick, and meanders through rolling
piedmont to the fall line near Laurel, and thence through the coastal
plain to the Chesapeake—a distance of more than one hundred miles.
The Patuxent is the longest river entirely within the state of Maryland,
and its drainage area occupies almost one-tenth of the state's total land
area. While the fall line is the head of navigation on most rivers, it never
was on the Patuxent. Even before the river started silting up, which oc-

curred shortly after the first settlers started clearing woods, ships could only go as far as Pig Point, a few miles above Upper Marlboro and roughly fifty miles from the Chesapeake.

The Patuxent River empties into the Chesapeake between Cove Point and Cedar Point. The latter is marked by an abandoned lighthouse; the lighthouse on the former, built in 1828, was one of the last lighthouses on the bay to be automated.

The nameless bay just inside the river's entrance is almost perfectly circular, two miles in diameter, and for the most part astonishingly deep—fifty, sixty, even eighty feet in places. The shore on the south side, near Fishing Point, is flat and low, the perfect site for an airfield; and in 1942 the U.S. Navy built the Patuxent River Naval Air Station here. More than half a century later, "Pax River" continues to dominate the sounds—and the economy—of southern Maryland. The high cliffs on the north shore, near Drum Point (which also had a lighthouse until two decades ago, when it was deactivated and moved to the Calvert Marine Museum, on Solomons Island), evoked a prophetic comment from a writer in the late 1880s: "Never have I seen more tempting building sites." The writer predicted that "for aquatic sports the harbor of the Patuxent would offer abundant facilities."

The "harbor of the Patuxent" eventually became an aquatic facility the nineteenth-century writer could hardly have imagined: a seaplane base that until recently operated on these waters. The "abundant facilities" did spring up, but not until the 1960s, and then in and around the protected harbor of Solomons Island.

"Solomon's Island, a village situated on the shores of an island of the same name and whose harbor draws forth encomiums of praise from all visitors," wrote George and Robert Barrie in *Cruises Mostly in the Bay of the Chesapeake,* published in 1909, "sleeps calmly on in the certainty that some day the natural advantages of the Patuxent mouth . . . will be realized."

First variously called Sandy Island and Somervell Island, the town, with its wonderfully protected harbor, took its current name from Isaac

Solomon, who bought the island and opened an oyster processing plant shortly after the Civil War. The first bridge to the island was built in 1870. Fishing, oystering, and boatbuilding sustained the economy. In 1919 the Chesapeake Biological Laboratory was opened, the oldest permanent state-supported marine biological laboratory in continuous use on the East Coast. Solomons remained a sleepy village even after the U.S. Navy arrived across the river in 1942 and a naval amphibious base was built to train thousands in the techniques of amphibious warfare, which many put into practice on the Solomon Islands, in the Pacific.

Solomons Island is likely to show up on many sailors' lists of favorite places. There are a half dozen anchorages on the creeks inside the harbor (although anchoring in the inner harbor is no longer permitted). There are many restaurants and marinas, and a fine museum. And who could resist sailing past a well-marked, triangular little island in the harbor, known as Molly's Legg? Local lore has it that Molly's Legg was the burial ground for unidentified bodies washed up on the shore. I was quite familiar with Molly's Legg, having once touched it, so to speak, when I ran hard aground in a deep-keel boat when I tried to enter Solomons, at night, for the first time many years ago.

But I decided not to go inside. Instead, I circumnavigated the circular roadstead. I tacked back and forth along the edge of the Patuxent Naval Air Station, with its radar towers, bulbous hangars, and air traffic control towers. Past the seaplane basins, no longer in use, I headed upriver, skirting the causeway that now connects Solomons with the mainland. Solomons offers a charming riverfront, with its Victorian church spires and a motley collection of carpenter-Gothic turn-of-the-century houses nestled against the several buildings of the Calvert Marine Museum.

A 140-foot-high, two-lane bridge links the counties that border the Patuxent: Calvert and Saint Marys. Like most bridges around the Chesapeake, it was named after a politician—Maryland's first elected governor, Thomas Johnson—when it was completed in 1972, but it was promptly and forever after called the Solomons Island bridge by the local populace. It would be wonderful if more bridges could be named after poets (New Jersey has its Walt Whitman Bridge) or explorers (New York has its Verrazano) — even perhaps, some day, Captain John Smith.

The unusual height of the Solomons Island bridge, a Navy dictate, is mirrored in the great depth of the Patuxent at nearby Point Patience: more than one hundred feet. Nevertheless, while looking for this information on my chart, I managed to run hard aground on the long sandbar off Point Patience which juts out into the river just above the bridge, and which I had elected to cut close in true Dovekie fashion. I immediately understood how the point got its name. It was not a serious matter, however, except that as I stepped from the boat onto terra firma I noticed a sign that said that I was trespassing on government property and would have to stay seventy-five yards away from shore. I wondered briefly about the seventy-five yards — 225 feet. Why not fifty yards, or one hundred? Who makes up these notions? I dragged *Fiddler* off the beach and back into the deep Patuxent. The water was warmer than the air. John Smith had noted its depth during his exploration. "The fifth river is called Pawtuxunt, and is of a lesse proportion then the rest; but the channell is 16 or 18 fadome deepe in some places."

It had breezed up to about twelve knots, still from the west, and that made for a fabulous, fast reach toward Mill Creek at Half Pone Point, one of three Mill Creeks on the Patuxent, and one of nearly a dozen on the Chesapeake. But this Mill Creek, although very sheltered from the breeze, was not the quiet gunkhole that the chart promised. A jumble of houses and piers lined the shore, and I jibed around to continue on toward Saint Leonards Creek, four miles further on the other side of the river, thought by many to be one of the prettiest deepwater anchorages in the bay. A large ketch, under sail, preceded me into the creek.

Saint Leonards Creek penetrates a narrow peninsula between the river and the Chesapeake, reaching to within a mile and a half of the latter, near the Calvert Cliffs power plant. The writer Paul Wilstach called it "a minor body of water of singular beauty." Rodney Point, near its mouth, hides the main stretch from the river. Its shores are frequently more than one hundred feet high, and here and there they come down to the water in steep bluffs. Just within its mouth Commodore Joshua Barney fought the so-called Battle of the Barges in the War of 1812.

Barney, a deep-water sailor and Revolutionary War privateer, was in command of a tiny collection of shallow-draft barges manned by five hundred "flotillamen," the only American Navy presence in the Chesapeake Bay. The bay was the center of the Royal Navy's attention. Much of America's export shipping came from its hundreds of harbors and rivers. Both Baltimore and Washington could be reached by large fighting ships, and the English armada consisted of four ships of the line, some twenty frigates and sloops, and more than twenty transports.

First, however, it would have to deal with Barney, "as aggressive a sailor as the U.S. had," according to one historian's description. Barney had first gone to sea at the age of twelve; in 1813 he was fifty-four years old. What would be his last command consisted of three small gunboats and thirteen pulling barges, with about five hundred men.

On June 1, 1813, the tiny fleet was en route to Tangier Island, in the middle of the bay, where the British earlier in the year had established a base. Near the mouth of the Patuxent, however, Barney encountered a British squadron commanded by Captain Robert Barrie. Outgunned, he escaped into the river, and then retreated into the shallower waters of Saint Leonards Creek. On three succeeding days a week later, the British, now using small barges and rocket boats, attacked the Americans, but were repulsed each time. At dawn on June 26, Barney was finally able to escape. Ten men had been killed or wounded, and the three gunboats had to be left behind. The remaining barges were moved, first to the village of Nottingham, thirty miles up the river, and then to Pig Point, near Upper Marlboro, more than forty miles above the mouth.

Nearly two months later, the British landed troops at Benedict and began their march on Washington. A search party of small boats was sent up the river, and on August 22 it found Barney's flotilla. Rear Admiral George Cockburn later reported to his superior:

On approaching Pig Point where the enemy's flotilla was said to be, I landed the Marines . . . then proceeded on with the boats, and as we opened the reach above Pig Point I plainly discovered Commodore Barney's broad pendant in the headmost vessel (a large sloop), and the remainder of the flotilla extending in a long line astern of her. Our boats now advanced towards them as rapidly as possible but on nearing them we observed the sloop bearing the broad pendant to be on fire, and she very soon afterwards blew up. I now saw clearly that they were all abandoned and on fire . . . out of the 17 vessels which composed this formidable and so much vaunted flotilla, 16 were in quick succession blown to atoms.

Barney had been ordered to destroy his fleet. He and his men fought valiantly at the Battle of Bladensburg to prevent the British troops from capturing Washington. During the battle, Commodore Barney was wounded and captured. The British torched the public buildings in Washington.

Saint Leonards Creek, too, seemed to have been captured and wounded, and I almost hoped that some of the private buildings along its banks could be torched. It had surrendered its pristine beauty to "progress," and it was not as undeveloped as it had looked at the entrance. There were many nooks, coves, and crannies, but nearly all had piers, or boathouses, and homes — most new, many still under construction. The houses, some of which were partly hidden in the trees on the high banks, were all clearly expensive. But the ones I could see were uninteresting, and some were just ugly. The creek, in my opinion, could no longer qualify for the high praise it had received from the *Cruising Guide to the Chesapeake:* "Beautiful enough to rival anything on the Chesapeake." A small marina and a yacht club were a mile or so up the creek and provided berths for yachts, but I saw only two cruising boats at anchor.

I anchored and lunched on chicken salad in a shallow, unnamed cove, protected from the wind and waves. After an hour's rest, I decided to sail on. It took nearly half an hour to tack, against the wind, out of the creek. At the entrance, several fishermen were trot-lining for crabs and appeared to be having a profitable afternoon.

Sixty years ago it was possible for Paul Wilstach to write, in *Tidewater Maryland*, "There is no established allure about the Patuxent River. It is little known. It is the most sparsely inhabited and least known, probably, of all the rivers of Tidewater Maryland. It is not in the pathway of any flow of human life. Neither commerce nor tourism has disturbed it. It is, indeed, the least disturbed or improved of any of the larger rivers on this side of the bay."

This was no longer true. Since then, the population in Calvert County alone had more than quadrupled, while farm acreage declined by more than 40 percent. Solomons Island acquired a Hilton Conference Center, and traffic proliferated as the highways to Washington, D.C., an hour's drive away, were improved. The water quality of the river did not, of course, improve. Overpopulation in urban areas north of the river's mouth had exceeded the river's capacity to cleanse itself. In 1977 an article in the *Baltimore Evening Sun* stated, "Steeped in sewage and laced with chlorine, the Patuxent, most of it still beautiful to the eye, is a conduit of toxic wastes of suburban growth."

As one contributor wrote in Paula Johnson's *Working the Water,* "The logical conclusion of the pessimistic prognosis twenty or even ten years ago was that the Patuxent, and probably the entire Chesapeake system, would be dead bodies of water" by the 1980s. Though the Patuxent in the 1990s is not dead, it is ailing. Sixty years ago there were no sewage treatment plants in the Patuxent watershed. Today ten plants together discharge more than 40 million gallons per day into the river, which miraculously still supports a small fishing industry and is still clean enough for swimming. Tom Horton and William Eichbaum reported in *Turning the Tide* that "the Patuxent, after a twenty-year decline, has begun to show a trend of improving water quality in its upper and middle portions."

The wind backed into the southwest, increased to about fifteen knots, and provided an exhilarating ride past Sotterley Point toward

Broomes Island, the site of a small fishing village, and no longer an island. But the beauty of the river was again marred by a particularly ugly conspiracy of houses built on the western edge of the marshy spit that is Broomes Island. As the Alliance for the Chesapeake Bay had pointed out: "Planners studying the land use changes that have spurred the river's decline have identified low-density residential sprawl as the principal factor promoting abusive land use." The horrendously bad taste of the homeowners was manifested by structures embodying the worst excesses of American architects and builders. I decided to pass Broomes Island up, and was glad when the development disappeared from sight behind my back.

The glorious weather had brought out four other sailboats, more than I'd seen at one time on any of my other river cruises. And the Patuxent's shores became lovely again. I passed up a few tempting anchorages and took advantage of the sensational breeze to gain some distance up the river. Although I probably was going no faster than six knots, we seemed to be planing. *Fiddler* almost sported a rooster tail, and air bubbles came boiling up from behind her rudder, whose lowered blade I could see through the unusually clear water. A half dozen cormorants sat drying their wings on fishing weir stakes off Jack Bay. I skirted Jack Bay's marsh, jibed, and ran into Battle Creek, past a prosperous-looking farm on Prison Point. Battle Creek is often mistakenly thought to be the site of the Battle of the Barges, but was in fact named after the town of Battel, in Sussex, England, the birthplace of one of the early immigrants. It was nearing four o'clock, and I poked up the creek to look for a pleasant and protected anchorage for the night.

I found it in a long cove called Long Cove, a half mile up the creek. Still moving at hull speed, I rounded up just inside the entrance; the rudder kicked up as I found myself in shallow water. Seconds later I was anchored in the lee of a high bank with huge trees. There wasn't a ripple on the water. There were a couple of houses at the far end of the cove; a small community pier with several small sailboats jutted out from the opposite shore. It was a pleasant and peaceful scene. The enormous trees that gave me protection from the wind blocked the rays of the late afternoon sun, and I soon changed into warmer clothes and reluctantly put on a pair of shoes, having forgotten to bring a pair of socks. The water was still warm, but I wasn't tempted to swim. The day's sail, mostly reaching and running, had been effortless, and I figured that I could go without bathing until the sun once again was high in the sky.

On the first day of my Patuxent cruise, *Fiddler* had taken me a dozen miles up the river. This late in the season there would be only a slight chance of bugs, but I lowered the mast and put up my tent anyway. It only took a few minutes, and the tent would help to keep me warm, for the temperature was sure to dip into the forties. I had managed to pick up scraps of the weather forecast. The southwesterly breeze presaged the arrival, in the morning, of what was called "a secondary reinforcing cold front," after which the winds would switch to the northwest (the direction I was headed) and deliver below-normal temperatures for several days. The good news was that there would be plenty of sunshine.

The early nightfall came as a bit of a shock: during my earlier cruises I had been used to daylight lasting well into my dinner hour. I barely had time to cook dinner before dusk descended on my tranquil world. When I slipped into my sleeping bag and tried to read, I discovered that the batteries in my reading light had given up the ghost. An hour later a full moon rose over the trees on the far side of the cove, but it was not bright enough to read by. The last thing I remembered before sliding into sleep was that the thermometer read forty-eight degrees and was still dropping.

I have been told that I sleep longer than most people. I need about nine hours of shut-eye, but after more than ten hours of darkness I was ready to greet the dawn. It was a blessing that this would be a sunny day! I needed the sun not only for light but also for warmth, and not just for myself. I needed the sun to help dry out the bottom of my sleeping bag, which had received a steady drip of dew during the night as the roof of my tent puckered and puddled. A cup or more had soaked the bag, and my feet had been cold.

I welcomed the dawn, as did hundreds of birds that simultaneously began to twitter and chirp. The leaves on the trees surrounding my anchorage were not moving; however, shards of mist were streaming past, still out of the southwest, also a welcome sign. The extent of the spit I had scraped while sailing into the cove the night before was now fully revealed, and I knew then (having once again forgotten the tide tables) the approximate time of low tide for this portion of the Patuxent.

Fiddler, of course, was no place to cook while under way. At anchor, her horseshoe-shaped stern seat became my kitchen, study, and navigation desk. On the starboard side there would be the dishwashing paraphernalia, brush, soap, and scrubber; next to these sat the two-burner propane stove, cooking utensils, and the ingredients of the meal to come; then the water jug. On the port side, the seat was usually occupied with charts, logbook, and whatever book I was currently reading—for most of the cruises it was Middleton's *Tobacco Coast.* Somehow I would manage to find a few square inches for myself on the port quarter. If the tent was up, this space had the most headroom, and I could even sit on a cushion. The scene was always one of wholesale confusion, but everything was within arm's reach. Before getting under way, I would stow everything in the storage bins forward, and the only things left in the cockpit would be a seat cushion, the chart, and my between-meal snacks—a small box of raisins and a plastic bottle of seltzer, both easily handled while under way.

The chilly weather called for a hot, hearty breakfast, and I took temporary leave from my diet of fat-free cereal and fruit. I scrambled corned beef hash, poached eggs, and burned toast. Because the manufacturers of corned beef hash are apparently not required to disclose the contents of their products, my guilt could be somewhat assuaged by my ignorance.

After meals, if the mast were down, I would rinse my dishes in water from a plastic solar shower bag that hung from the spar, its hose just outside the cockpit. If the day had been sunny, the dinner dishes would be rinsed in hot water. The breakfast dishes, naturally, were always rinsed in cold.

When the sun finally cleared the trees at the end of Long Cove, it was nearly 7:30, and when the light hit the trees on the banks around the cove, some of them seemed to have changed into their fall costume overnight. I was not in a hurry to leave. First, things would have to dry out before I could put the tent away. And it would be nice if things could warm up before *Fiddler* and I got out in the breeze.

My plan for the day was unambitious. I wanted to move another dozen miles or so closer to the head of navigation, and I planned to stop at Benedict, a small town at the next bridge over the Patuxent, only a half dozen miles upstream, to see if batteries could be found for my reading light. Benedict was the last town I would pass on the river where there might be a store.

By 9:30 I was ready to leave, and the wind had already shifted into the northwest. What with the full moon and the low tide, I managed to hit bottom a few times on my way out of the Battle Creek into the river. The really shallow places were occupied by scores of wading birds looking for food, and it was easy to avoid them.

The wind on the river was brisk, and right on the nose. But I welcomed this for a change, for here the river was still wide enough to tack; by the time the wind shifted into the south again, as it inevitably would, I would presumably be in the narrower portion of the river, where tacking might be impossible.

As soon as I was out on the river, I could see the bridge at Benedict on the horizon, and behind it the seven tall stacks of the Pepco power plant at Chalk Point. They would dominate the landscape of the Patuxent for most of the day. But the shore on both sides of the river was beautiful, with meadows sloping down to the water between bold cliffs. There were few houses.

Fiddler is not exactly a stunning performer while going to windward in a choppy sea, and with the current foul it took nearly two hours

to reach Benedict. The wind blew hard, straight down the river, sometimes gusting to speeds that made me think of reefing. The old adage
"Never belay the mainsheet on a small boat" was never more worth re-
membering. Time after time I had to spill the wind out of the sail to
keep the boat upright.

The little town of Benedict was named for the fourth Lord Baltimore. It was here that the British disembarked in August 1814 to begin
their march on Washington, where they fired the Capitol. The Patuxent off Benedict is still more than 30 feet deep. A swing bridge, the
only crossing on the tidal portion of the river until the Thomas Johnson
bridge was opened in 1972, spans the river between Town Point and Hallowing Point. (There are several Hallowing Points at narrow spots on
rivers around the Chesapeake Bay; the name is thought to stem from the
"hollering" people did to catch the attention of a ferryman or a pilot.)

At Benedict I went ashore after tying *Fiddler* to a pier between
two of the several restaurants on the waterfront. Across the street, staff
members of the Benedict Estuarine Research Laboratory were having
lunch around a picnic table in front of their research station. The laboratory, part of the Academy of Natural Sciences, was founded in 1967 and
carries on research on many aspects of marine life in the Chesapeake.
With a staff of thirty-five and an annual operating budget of $1 million,
it is the largest employer in Benedict. I asked for directions to a nearby
store, and then walked to the only store in town, a small grocery several
blocks from the waterfront, where I discovered that C batteries were
not carried. I would not be reading after dark.

The lunch special at one of the restaurants was softshell crabs, and
I succumbed to the temptation. From a riverside table I watched *Fiddler*
while I devoured several of the delicacies. After the meal I boarded
the Dovekie, lowered the mast to scoot under the bridge, motored to
the other side, raised mast and sail, and headed for Gods Grace Point,
opposite the power plant; the wind was still plentiful and gusty.

Adjoining the Pepco plant was the rich-sounding but poor-looking
subdivision of Eagle Harbor. Further upriver on the opposite shore, near

Holland Cliff, another development appeared, this one looking suspiciously like condominiums.

The Patuxent narrowed to one-fifth of a mile. At Holland Cliff I passed red marker number 28, the last navigational buoy. Almost immediately the scenery improved once again. For as far as I could see, there was only water, woods, meadows, and marshes, with a good-looking barn the only evidence of a human presence. Of this natural beauty a British officer wrote during the War of 1812, calling it "the most delightful mixture of art and nature that can possibly be conceived."

By late afternoon I was nearly thirty miles up the Patuxent and confronted with a choice of anchorages at a bend in the river. On the west side a narrow, shallow stream called Black Swamp Creek looked inviting, but on the east side a far more serpentine creek called Cocktown Creek beckoned. The latter seemed to offer more shelter from the possible thunderstorms that were mentioned in the fragments of forecasts I was able to receive.

Cocktown Creek's entrance was very shoal, but a few hundred feet up the stream, where it was just wide enough to turn *Fiddler* around, I found a five-foot spot—deep enough to swim—where I dropped anchor. I barely had swinging room, but my anchorage was completely protected, placid, and private.

I swam in the warm, fresh water. If the weather was going to be as cold as predicted for the next few days, this would be my last swim of the year. By the end of my journey up the Patuxent I would be more than 120 miles further north than my starting point, earlier in the year, at the mouth of the James.

With dusk rapidly approaching, dinner was a hasty affair, and twenty minutes after the brilliant sunset I stuffed myself into my sleeping bag. Even if I had found batteries for my reading light they would not have seen any use. I fell asleep waiting for the full moon to come up.

I woke shortly after midnight. A light rain was falling. The moon, unseen behind the clouds, was undoubtedly full, but the creek was undoubtedly empty. *Fiddler* sat on the bottom. Except for the spot where I'd been swimming, and where the anchor presumably still was hooked to the bottom, there was no water left in the creek. The hard winds and the full moon had teamed up and left me high and dry. Although I probably wouldn't have been so foolhardy as to even attempt this creek in a keelboat, I was glad that the Dovekie was as upright aground as she was afloat.

It rained intermittently during the night. "Their Rains, except in the depth of Winter, are extreamly agreeable and refreshing," Robert Beverley had written in the early 1700s. "All the Summer long they last but a few Hours at a time." Around two the rain stopped. Around three I felt *Fiddler* move again. Groggily I calculated that I would have to move back into deeper water no later than 10 A.M. in order not to get stuck again, then fell asleep once more.

Dawn came slow, gray, and reluctant. There had been little wind during the night, so no rainwater had found its way through the screened windows of the tent into the boat, but the fabric still leaked in places, and I was happy to see the gray skies begin to break up an hour after dawn.

Insofar as was possible I got dressed while still in the sleeping bag, and again rued the fact that I had forgotten to bring socks. Cranking up the stove to make coffee helped to heat things up a bit in the cockpit, and the lack of wind was now a blessing. My pan from dinner the night before came up spic and span. Even this far north, and this late in the season, the crabs were still doing their excellent scavenging.

After breakfast I moved the boat out of the narrow creek back into the river and into depths of a few feet instead of a few inches of water. It was too shallow to row, or scull, or motor, and too muddy to pole or walk the boat out. The motor would probably suck up more mud than water at these shallow depths, so standing up in the forward hatch I used a small canoe paddle that I kept for close-quarters maneuvering to move *Fiddler* the few hundred feet into deeper water. It was not easy to turn the boat around in the narrow, muddy little ditch. I hadn't realized how, even at high tide yesterday, I'd been plain lucky to find whatever channel there was, for it now took a number of attempts before I found enough depth to lower the rudder and get ready to sail.

The current in the river appeared to have several hours of further ebbing ahead, and I elected to wait until it turned. This was likely to be my last full day on the Patuxent, and with strong winds again forecast to be on the nose the whole day, I did not need to be saddled with adverse currents.

They say, "Reef early." Well, by 8 A.M. I had tucked in a reef and I was still at anchor. There wasn't a breath of air, but the forecast, which I now received clearly (since I was now less than twenty miles from Washington's Capital Beltway), kept insisting that the wind would go to twenty knots at any minute. It was funny to listen to those forecasts while sitting at anchor on the edge of the river with my reefed sail hanging listlessly from the mast, but since I was not in any great hurry I decided to await the unfolding events.

Ten minutes later I was glad I had reefed while things were still calm. The cold front had arrived. The wind edged toward its promised velocity, the last of the clouds were blown eastward, and I weighed anchor. But half an hour later I was still less than a half mile from my starting point: the current was still too strong, and I couldn't stem the tide.

The strenuous and demanding sailing was keeping me warm, however, and the scenery, hardly moving even at my ever-so-slightly-improving speed, was incomparable. Near noon I had managed to reach Lower Marlboro, two miles from my morning's starting point. Here the river began to twist and turn, often presenting me with better sailing angles than the beats I had to sail from Cocktown Creek. And the current, of course, slowly reversed itself as the morning wore on. It would be favoring me the rest of the day.

At Lower Marlboro, described as "a modest village" a century ago, the Patuxent narrows appreciably, to less than a tenth of a mile. Still, the water has depths of thirty, and sometimes even forty, feet. Marshes alternated at each of the "curles" with hills on both sides—some more than one hundred feet high. A few good-looking houses and some decrepit-looking bungalows bordered the river at Lower Marlboro—the better houses were up on the hill, the shacks on the water. There was no landing or pier to tempt the sailor to come ashore.

At Short Point, just beyond Lower Marlboro, I was forcefully reminded that the outside turns of waterways, having a greater current velocity, carry the deepest water. *Fiddler's* rudder kicked up as I tried to plow through less than two feet of water on the inside turn and frightened a great blue heron into flight.

The Patuxent was giving me some of the best sails of my various river cruises. There was less wind in the lee of White Landing, another tiny settlement; I shook the reef out of the sail and then sailed around the next point, right off my chart. The rest of the voyage would be made without the benefit of cartography. When I realized that I would have little shelter in the miles ahead, I turned back to my marshy lee, anchored, made a sandwich for lunch, and napped in the cockpit, out of the breeze and with the sun warming me.

Nottingham, once a village but now a tiny, jumbled subdivision thirty-three miles from the mouth of the Patuxent, still had depths of more than thirty feet along its waterfront, according to the *Coast Pilot,* but from here northward, the river had silted up considerably, a process that was noted by the early colonists soon after they began the deforestation and cultivation of land upstream. In 1888, silt buildup prompted the dredging of the river to a depth of nine feet as far as Bristol Landing, ten miles above Nottingham, which was then still an important tobacco shipping point. In a study concluded ten years ago, researchers found that on average, 710,600 *tons* of dirt was still washing into the river each year.

From Nottingham to Patuxent River Park at Jug Bay, a distance of about six miles, the river meandered through mile-wide marshes, but fortunately the channel was marked with red and green floating buoys, which I assumed had been placed by the park rangers. Although the

current was still flooding, the water level was in fact falling, a phenome-
non I have never understood. Low tide was near, and the mudflats were
covered with foraging wading birds.

With the channel now less than one hundred feet wide, it became
impossible to beat to windward in the breeze, which was sometimes still
gusting to twenty knots. I had wanted to finish my voyage under sail, but
a half mile from the park, with the ramp in sight, I reluctantly rolled up
Fiddler's red sail and started the engine.

My Dovekie's water-jet engine has neither neutral nor reverse set-
tings. When the engine starts, the boat moves ahead, although slowly
at first. The choppy water and the brisk breeze made my landing alongside the wharf at Jackson's Landing less than seamanlike. Just before I
reached the little fishing pier, I shut the engine down to allow the little
ship to coast to a stop, and crawled forward along the boat's bottom to
the forward hatch, where I emerged to fend *Fiddler* off. I found myself
inches away from the face of a little girl in a big orange life jacket who
was fishing from the edge of the pier. I'm not sure which of us was more
surprised, but she recovered quickly.

"Did you have a nice day?" she inquired.

"A very nice day," I said, as I looped my bowline over a piling. "A
very nice day."

The cruise was not quite over, however. I wanted to sail as far as
Pig Point (where Commodore Barney had destroyed his flotilla), which
was the head of navigation nearly two hundred years ago. And I wouldn't
be met with the trailer until early the next day. But first I wanted to
stretch my legs.

I left the boat alongside the fishing pier and went for a walk through
part of the two-thousand-acre Jug Bay Natural Area, which has hiking
trails, historical and archaeological exhibits, camping and canoeing ac-
tivities, and opportunities for nature study around the wetlands. At last
count 254 species of birds had been sighted at the park, and it had
been confirmed that birds of 97 species, including a pair of bald eagles,
nested there.

When in late afternoon I returned to the landing, the wind had died down considerably. I cast off my lines and then sailed a mile or so further up the river, past the Patuxent's Western Branch, now almost totally silted up, which led to Upper Marlboro.

Upper Marlboro, named after the duke of Marlborough, was laid out in 1706 and became a community of regional importance long before the Revolutionary War. But as early as 1739 there were complaints about the shoaling of the Western Branch. The town was, and is, a tobacco mart of some consequence. At the tobacco warehouses alongside the Western Branch, the leaf was put on lighters and poled three miles to the Patuxent proper. There it was transferred to vessels that carried it to the English markets. By the middle of the eighteenth century the Patuxent had lost eight miles of navigable length and had lost perhaps as much as seven feet of water depth.

I sailed, then rowed, another mile up the river. On the east side, on a high bluff, was a motley collection of a dozen or so small cottages: Pig Point had become Bristol Landing. No piers marred the river's edge. The channel was still easily deep enough for *Fiddler*. Wild rice dominated the mile-wide marsh. In the reach beyond Pig Point there was no evidence of Commodore Barney's flotilla, although the Calvert Marine Museum in Solomons has several displays of parts of barges which were recovered by divers.

It was getting dark. I had no doubt that on another day, with *Fiddler's* mast down (and perhaps with the aid of a chainsaw) I could make my way as far as Route 50, and maybe beyond, to the fall line, another dozen miles.

Now, however, the cruise was coming to an end. I rowed back to the confluence of the Patuxent and its Western Branch, and anchored. I had not seen another boat since leaving Benedict, and I felt confident that none would appear now. My anchorage was gorgeous. Two mansions, one close to the river, the other up on a hill a mile to the north, were the only signs of civilization.

Well, not quite the only ones. I had started my cruises on the James with the deafening noise of helicopters overhead, and I was now finishing my cruise on the Patuxent in a spot located precisely underneath the Andrews Air Force Base flight pattern.

The nearly full moon rose within minutes of sunset, and soon afterward the temperature plummeted. Fortunately, not a trace was left of the near gale I had battled most of the day. *Fiddler* swung sideways with the reversing current until her stern scraped bottom near the edge. I cooked—or rather, heated—a quick dinner. The moonlight illuminated the fog that formed around my small world. After dinner I stuck my bare feet into the arms of an old woolen sweater and burrowed into my sleeping bag, fully clothed. I vaguely remember that the boat seemed to be aground, perhaps early in the morning, but there was no chance that I would get out of the sleeping bag to verify something so unimportant.

Dawn was particularly eerie. We were suspended in a low cloud. Even within the cockpit tent, my breath contributed significantly to the heavy fog outside. I stayed in my sleeping bag while I rummaged around for the makings of breakfast. There was frost on my propane bottle. By seven it was light enough for me to see what I was eating, and soon afterward I welcomed the sun, a golden disc rising above the still-invisible horizon.

Fiddler was afloat, but I had to push her stern away from the butterweed and wild rice on the edge of the river until she had swung back into the current. The time had come to put *Fiddler* away for the winter and start dreaming about sailing adventures in warmer climates. But all the discomfort of the cold disappeared as I rowed on a glassy river through the gray, misty landscape. Half an hour later the marshes of the Patuxent were revealed as the heat of the sun dissolved the last of the fog. *Fiddler's* trailer was waiting at Jug Bay.

Afterword

"When you drive," wrote Franklin Burroughs in a book about the Waccamaw River, "the road defines the landscape, which becomes only the soiled and slovenly corridor through which you move, a measurement of the time you have passed and the time that lies ahead of you. But rivers both define and express a landscape, and they do it slowly, organically, and profoundly, the way a history defines and expresses a culture."

My favorite word in this thoughtful passage is "slowly," for it, more than anything else, helped define my treks up the rivers. The total distance that I traveled, roughly four hundred miles, could be covered in a day by many of today's speedboats or "personal watercraft" (as the pesky jet skis are now called), many of which can, and unfortunately do, travel at fifty miles per hour. But what glories a high-speed traveler would miss!

Thoreau, as *A Week on the Concord and Merrimack Rivers* makes clear, loved rivers. "They are the constant lure, when they flow by our doors, to distant enterprise and adventure," he noted. It was remarkable to me how in the closing decade of the twentieth century it was still possible — and easy — to find solitude and adventure in an area that is said to be within a day's drive of half the population of the United States.

"Travel," Paul Theroux wrote, "has less to do with distance than with insight; it is, very often, a way of seeing." And traveling at a couple of miles per hour, as one does in a small sailing — or rowing — boat, allows one to see the landscape more clearly. There are more than 250 public access boat ramps scattered around the Chesapeake and its myriad tributaries. A small boat, a few hours, and some decent weather can provide all the ingredients for an adventure not far from home.

Like Huck Finn, "we had mighty good weather as a general thing, and nothing ever happened to us at all." The most remarkable thing about my time on the rivers was the absence of people. Except on the few weekends that I spent on the rivers, and then only in the most benevolent of weather conditions, people using the rivers, either for work or for recreation, were a rarity.

Jonathan Raban, in *Coasting,* wrote: "Seeing what you like. . . . sailing along on any damn-fool course you choose, you are—weather permitting—as liberated a spirit as any human being on the face of the globe." Nearly half a million boats are registered in Maryland and Virginia, but only the tiniest percentage choose to explore in this way. And it doesn't require an ultra-shoal-draft vessel like *Fiddler.* With few exceptions, larger and deeper-draft boats can explore nearly all parts of these waterways.

As we approach the four-hundredth anniversary of the founding of the first permanent settlement on the Chesapeake, it is my fondest wish that these five fair rivers will not deteriorate further; even, that water quality and responsible land use will improve. After all, I plan to take my grandchildren on some grand cruises.

SOME PLEASANT READING

Barbour, Philip L. *The Three Worlds of Captain John Smith.* Boston: Houghton Mifflin, 1964.

Barrie, George, Jr., and Robert Barrie. *Cruises Mainly in the Bay of the Chesapeake.* Bryn Mawr, Pa.: Franklin, 1909.

Beitzell, Edwin W. *Life on the Potomac River.* Washington, D.C.: By the author, 1968.

Byron, Gilbert. *The War of 1812 on the Chesapeake Bay.* Baltimore: Maryland Historical Society, 1964.

Capper, John, et al. *Chesapeake Waters: Pollution, Public Health, and Public Opinion, 1607–1972.* Centreville, Md.: Tidewater, 1983.

Chesterman, W. D. *The James River Tourist.* Richmond, Va.: Tatum, 1899.

de Gast, Robert. *The Lighthouses of the Chesapeake.* Baltimore: Johns Hopkins University Press, 1973.

Earle, Swepson. *The Chesapeake Bay Country.* Baltimore: Thomson-Ellis, 1923.

Footner, Hulbert. *Sailor of Fortune: The Life and Adventures of Commodore Barney, U.S.N.* New York: Harper and Brothers, 1940.

Gutheim, Frederick. *The Potomac.* New York: Rinehart, 1949.

Hall, Clayton Colman, ed. *Narratives of Early Maryland.* New York: Scribner's Sons, 1910.

Horton, Tom, and William M. Eichbaum. *Turning the Tide: Saving the Chesapeake Bay.* Washington, D.C.: Island, 1991.

Hutchins, Frank. *Virginia, the Old Dominion.* Boston: Page, 1921.

Hutchins, Frank, and Cortelle Hutchins. *Houseboating on a Colonial Waterway.* Boston: Page, 1910.

Johnson, Paula J., ed. *Working the Water.* Charlottesville: University Press of Virginia, 1988.

Kauffman, John M. *Flow East: A Look at Our North American Rivers.* New York: McGraw-Hill, 1973.

Lewis, C. M., and A. J. Loomie. *The Spanish Jesuit Mission in Virginia, 1570–1572.* Chapel Hill: University of North Carolina Press, 1953.

Metcalf, Paul. *Waters of Potowmack.* San Francisco: North Point, 1982.

Middleton, Arthur Pierce. *Tobacco Coast: A Maritime History of Chesapeake Bay in the Colonial Era.* Baltimore: Johns Hopkins University Press, 1984.

Niles, Blair. *The James.* New York: Farrar and Rinehart, 1939.

Rothrock, J. T. *Vacation Cruising in Chesapeake and Delaware Bays.* Philadelphia: Lippincott, 1884.

Stone, Roger D. *The Voyage of the Sanderling.* New York: Knopf, 1990.

Stone, William T., and Fessenden S. Blanchard. *A Cruising Guide to the Chesapeake.* New York: Dodd, Mead, 1973.

Stranahan, Susan Q. *Susquehanna, River of Dreams.* Baltimore: Johns Hopkins University Press, 1993.

Tate, Thad W., and David L. Ammerman. *The Chesapeake in the Seventeenth Century.* Chapel Hill: University of North Carolina Press, 1979.

Tilp, Frederick. *This Was Potomac River.* Alexandria, Va.: By the author, 1978.

———. *The Chesapeake Bay of Yore.* Alexandria, Va.: By the author, 1982.

Tyler, Lyon G., ed. *Narratives of Early Virginia, 1606–1625.* New York: Barnes and Noble, 1966.

Warner, William W. *Beautiful Swimmers: Watermen, Crabs, and the Chesapeake Bay.* Boston: Little, Brown, 1976.

Wilstach, Paul. *Potomac Landings.* Indianapolis: Bobbs-Merrill, 1932.

———. *Tidewater Maryland.* Cambridge, Md.: Tidewater, 1969.

———. *Tidewater Virginia.* Indianapolis: Bobbs-Merrill, 1929.

Woodlief, Ann. *In River Time: The Way of the James.* Chapel Hill, N.C.: Algonquin, 1985.

ACKNOWLEDGMENTS

Many people helped make the cruises—and the book—possible, provided encouragement or advice, shuttled *Fiddler*'s trailer, located the obscure book, maneuvered the manuscript. I particularly thank Robert Brugger, Jack Goellner, and Miriam Kleiger of the Johns Hopkins University Press, as well as Linda Gayle, Wil van Werkhoven, Andrew Teeling, Bill Tatum, Bill Nelson, Evelyn de Gast, Shelby Creagh, Ken Menzies, Carter Naeny, Justin de Gast, John Barth, and the staff of the Eastern Shore Public Library in Accomac, Virginia.

Library of Congress Cataloging-in-Publication Data

De Gast, Robert, 1936–
    Five fair rivers : sailing the James, York, Rappahannock, Potomac,
and Patuxent / Robert de Gast.
        p.   cm.
    Includes bibliographical references (p.   ).
    ISBN 0-8018-5079-7
    1. Rivers—Virginia.   2. Rivers—Maryland.   3. Virginia—
Description and travel.   4. Maryland—Description and travel.
I. Title.   II. Title: 5 fair rivers.
F232.A17D44   1995
917.5504'43—dc20   94-47377